FIELD DAYS

FIELD DAYS

JOURNAL OF AN ITINERANT BIOLOGIST

Roger B. Swain

CHARLES SCRIBNER'S SONS · NEW YORK

For Elisabeth,
with whom these stories begin and end.

Copyright © 1980, 1981, 1982, 1983 Roger B. Swain

Library of Congress Cataloging in Publication Data
Swain, Roger B.
  Field days.

  Bibliography: p.
  Includes index.
  1. Biology—Addresses, essays, lectures.
  2. Horticulture—Addresses, essays, lectures.
  3. Man—Influence on nature—Addresses, essays,
  lectures.   I. Title.
  QH311.S93   1983   574   83–11507
  ISBN 0–684–17989–X

1 3 5 7 9 11 13 15 17 19   F/C   20 18 16 14 12 10 8 6 4 2

Printed in the United States of America.

"Northern Comfort," "Spring Time," "Gypsy Moths," and "A Drink You Can Swim In" were first published in The New York Times Magazine; *"Bare Harvard" and "The Ungracious Host" in* Discover; *"Sophisticated Flypaper" and "Inhouse Outhouse" in* Technology Illustrated. *All other essays except "Captain's Log," previously unpublished, first appeared in* Horticulture.

CONTENTS

1	FIREWOOD	*1*
2	AVOCADOS	*9*
3	WHITE BLOOMERS	*16*
4	NORTHERN COMFORT	*26*
5	GUESTS AT WORK	*36*
6	SPRING TIME	*44*
7	CROWBARS, GLACIERS, AND ZEN TEMPLES	*55*
8	GYPSY MOTHS	*64*
9	BARE HARVARD	*79*
10	MULBERRY VISIONS	*86*
11	BEE BITES	*96*
12	A DRINK YOU CAN SWIM IN	*104*
13	TRACKSIDE	*117*
14	SOPHISTICATED FLYPAPER	*123*
15	ILL WINDS	*133*
16	FAIR DAYS FOR VEGETABLES	*143*
17	SEVEN STEPS TO A BETTER BOUNCE	*152*
18	MYCOLOGICAL	*165*
19	INHOUSE OUTHOUSE	*175*
20	THE UNGRACIOUS HOST	*180*
21	THE LAST POINSETTIA OF SUMMER	*189*
22	HAMBURGERS AND HOUSEPLANTS	*196*
23	CAPTAIN'S LOG	*203*
	FURTHER READING	*207*
	INDEX	*212*

"A traveller should be a botanist, for in all views plants form the chief embellishment."—CHARLES DARWIN

I

FIREWOOD

Grandfather holds up his pants with a piece of string. He has a belt somewhere, but he has lots more string—from bakery boxes, packages that came in the mail, bales of hay. It is all unknotted, rolled up, saved, and eventually reused to lengthen a clothesline, to splint a cracked chair rung, even to gather up firewood.

Fascinated by a man who is knotted instead of buckled, his grandson follows him across the broad side lawn of the farm into the maple woods. There the two of them collect dead branches, breaking them into short, even lengths. When they have a pile, they tie the sticks into a tight bundle with a piece of string, and carry the bundle back to the house, down the kitchen stairs, and add it to the pile of firewood behind the fruit-room door.

Years later, as the boy learns to use a hatchet and then an axe, he cuts thicker firewood, chopping up branches that are too thick to break just by stepping on them. Sometimes he chops down small trees, shouting, "Timber!" when they fall. The small sticks his grandfather still gathers have become kindling, not real firewood.

Today he owns a chain saw and in a few noisy, smoky, vibration-filled minutes, he can cut down a tree two feet in diameter. A tree that big contains a cord and a half of wood —a good part of the winter's wood supply. And he cuts it in a fraction of the time it takes his grandfather to pick up an equal amount of sticks.

All his friends have chain saws. Even those who have discovered that it doesn't take a 24-inch-long blade to cut down a 24-inch-diameter tree are buying bigger chain saws to speed up their firewood cutting. There is no place for an old man and his used string in a modern forest, where men safely swaddled in earmuffs, face shields, and cut-proof pants rip down trees, their two-cycle engines shattering the Sunday silence.

Cutting down a big tree has become easy, but a tree two feet in diameter, even when it is sawn into short lengths, won't fit into a wood stove. It must be split. Driving steel wedges with a sledgehammer takes the build of a blacksmith, the spirit of a gandy dancer. No one likes splitting wood for very long. Those who have split the most are the ones who crowd around demonstrations of mechanical wood splitters at county fairs, watching the fat, shiny, hydraulic piston advance and retreat, each time easily dividing a log in two. Mesmerized by a machine that does so easily what each of them has struggled with, the spectators have only two questions: "How much does it cost?" they ask the demonstrator, and "Couldn't I build one like that myself?" they ask themselves.

None of them question whether the logs need to be split, for logs that size can't be burned otherwise. But do the logs need to be split, or rather, should we be splitting logs? Foresters are alarmed when they see a truckload of cordwood cut from large trees. In the northeastern United States, foresters warn us, there won't be any trees left for lumber if all the prime sawlogs are thoughtlessly butchered into 16-inch lengths. The big trees, with straight, sound boles, should be sawn into boards—made into steaks, not ground beef.

Even if splitting logs isn't squandering board feet of lumber, it is wasting energy when you consider how difficult it is to pass a huge log through the door of a wood stove. Splitting wood with sledges and wedges, with a splitting maul, or with (heaven forbid) an axe is good exercise that quickly becomes exhausting. If you have a mechanical log splitter, you must count not only the cost of the gasoline, but the energy used in the manufacture of the machine itself, the steel, the aluminum, the rubber.

By the time you have reduced a log to firewood, the firewood gathered by grandfather looks pretty good. The so-called kindling looks as if it might serve as a main course for a fire, not just the appetizer. Gathering up sticks may take a little more time, but it takes a lot less energy and hardly any strength.

In New England, where the pastures have grown up to trees, where stone walls now lead off into the forest, there is such an abundance of wood that it is easy to understand how people get lost in it and end up wishing they could afford a mechanical log splitter. There is simply so much vegetation that people can't see clear to the economies.

In the rest of the world, however, where the forests are still being converted to pastures, if not deserts, wood is in short supply. The scarcity is a lot more serious than a lack of bean poles for the garden. There is not enough wood to cook food and keep warm. The problem is most serious in the countries of the Indian subcontinent, central Africa south of the Sahara, the Andes of South America, Central America, and the Caribbean. Firewood is now more than a day's walk from Katmandu if you gather it yourself, and a quarter of a family's yearly income if you buy it in town in Niger. Industrial nations dominate the world news with concern over the oil and coal supply, but scarcely any printer's ink is used to chronicle a much more serious energy shortage: the daily concern of the two billion people who do 90 percent of their cooking and heating with wood or charcoal.

The late Mao Zedong said, "Forestry supports agriculture." What he meant was that an adequate food supply without a means to cook it is a tin can without a can opener. A shortage of wood not only makes it difficult to digest what food there is, but it may reduce the harvest itself. In India, Pakistan, Bangladesh, and a great many countries where firewood is scarce or nonexistent, people are burning dried dung. This generates heat but at the same time it deprives cropland of essential nutrients and organic matter. India's National Commission on Agriculture has gone so far as to declare that the use of cow dung as a source of noncommercial fuel is virtually a crime.

In an effort to conserve existing supplies of firewood, stove designers everywhere are experimenting with more efficient cooking stoves. These stoves, simple in design and built from locally abundant materials like sand, clay, and old beer cans, focus the flames on the cooking surface. The pots are arranged to fit tightly, and in such a way that hot gases flow around them. The aim of the designers is to produce an inexpensive stove with an overall fuel efficiency of 20 to 30 percent, reducing the current wood requirement five- to tenfold.

With an increasing global population, however, conservation will not be enough. More firewood needs to be grown, and this means both better management of existing forests and the planting of new ones. Massive reforestation programs are easy to design and difficult to implement. The obstacles that must be overcome range from politics to herds of cattle, sheep, and goats that will destroy any newly planted seedlings. But firewood can be grown as a crop, and on land that is too rocky, too wet, or too steep for conventional agriculture.

The choice of which kind of trees to grow for firewood will depend on the site, but, in general, the trees will be pioneer species, the kind that grow up following a forest fire or landslide. Since the bare expanses of land created by man and his animals are as desolate as any created by a natural disaster, the colonists need to be as vigorous and adaptable as possible. Some of the trees, like alder and various legumes, will be ones that can fix their own nitrogen. Others, like ailanthus, will be trees that grow so vigorously we call them weeds. Most important, they will be species that regenerate rapidly and spontaneously after they are cut for firewood.

Anyone who has tried to get rid of a red maple by cutting it down knows that it won't work. You can cut the tree down to the ground and mow over it repeatedly, and the tree keeps sending up sprouts from the stump. When you are trying to make a clearing in the woods, this endless sprouting can drive you to herbicide. Ignore the sprouts and in a few years you have woods again, a dense thicket of many small trunks.

Nineteenth-century Victorian novels are full of such thickets, or coppices, as they were called. Since then, most people have forgotten exactly what the word means, but it is coming back into common usage. In the last year both the National Academy of Sciences and the *Next Whole Earth Catalog* have expounded on the virtues of coppicing as a way to solve the world's energy crisis.

If you want to grow trees for firewood, they should be ones that coppice well; that is, they should grow rapidly from stump sprouts or root suckers once the original tree has been cut down.

Given enough time, say, sixty to one hundred years, a coppice will come to resemble an ordinary wood, most of the trunks having been shaded out and killed by a few especially vigorous ones. Traditionally, however, a coppice is harvested every five to twenty years, at a time when the cutting yields a lot of small poles. While it takes only one tree, 21 inches in diameter at breast height, to supply a cord of firewood, it takes ninety trees if each measures only 3 inches. Nevertheless, a coppice of aspen after ten years of growth may contain five thousand such poles in an acre, or about fifty cords of firewood.

Many tree species coppice well: among northern temperate species, white ash, aspen, basswood (*Tilia*), black locust, chestnut, maple, oak, and tulip tree (*Liriodendron*). How often the trees are cut depends in part on the species. Willows for basketmaking are cut annually. For other trees, ten years is a common rotation. Some living trees have been cut down every decade for more than three centuries.

Coppice regrowth is harvested in the dormant season if possible, from three weeks after leaf fall to six weeks before bud break. Cuts are sloping and made close to the ground because a smooth, slanted cut sheds water, and the sprouts that arise from the root collar at or below the ground surface are the most vigorous and the least susceptible to rot.

In places where grazing animals might devour the new shoots, a modified cutting technique called pollarding is used. Here the original trunk is cut 4 to 12 feet above the ground and a cluster of sprouts develops at that height. These, in turn, are cut every fifteen years or less to prevent their becoming so thick that they break off and damage the pollard head. The trunks that remain can be used as living fence posts.

Coppicing is an ancient method of tree management going back in Europe some three thousand years to the Neolithic Age. In Great Britain, woodsmen managed coppices for the production of poles, firewood, and small wood for fences. Foresters, on the other hand, managed large trees for lumber. At a time when "by hook or by crook" referred to the right to gather whatever dead wood could be pulled down with a stick, the woodsman was more important than the forester. In the United States, oak and chestnut were once coppiced to produce charcoal. Before the widespread use of coal, whole hillsides were cut, or "coaled," for making iron and steel.

There are three advantages to coppicing. First, it eliminates the need to plant a new seedling for each tree that is cut down. At the time a trunk is cut, there is a well-established root system that will hold the soil on steep slopes and thus prevent erosion, and will also feed the new sprouts, permitting their rapid growth.

Second, by concentrating the crop in that period of the tree's life cycle when growth is most rapid, the annual production of wood from a given area reaches a maximum. Whereas an unmanaged forest may produce as little as a ton of dry firewood per acre per year, a well-managed coppice will produce ten times that. A family of four needs about 0.9 tons of firewood for cooking each year, and in a well-managed coppice that much firewood can be grown in an area 65 feet on a side. Some tree species have given even higher yields. Chestnut coppices in England have yielded 18 tons per acre per year, and the tropical legume tree *Leucaena leucocephala* has yielded 40 tons.

Finally, wood that is harvested after no more than a couple of decades is conveniently small. Critics will claim that much of it is brushwood, too small to burn. But they are the kind of people who own log splitters and advocate using giant machines to chop up whole trees to burn in power plants. Small wood is convenient. It doesn't require a chain saw to cut it down or cut it up. It doesn't need splitting. It dries rapidly. And you can tie up bundles of it with string.

Coppicing is sure to become an established practice wherever firewood plantations are established. But as long as half the wood being cut is still being used for cooking and heating, why should coppicing be relegated to Timbuktu? Even in the industrialized countries, people are returning to wood as a source of heat. The advantages of coppicing are the same in everyone's backyard, temperate or tropical, underdeveloped or overdeveloped. Grandfather, of course, must have known this all along: neatly tied bundles of firewood economize on more than string.

2

AVOCADOS

Under the abandoned avocado tree, pits cover the ground as thickly as golf balls at a driving range. Some have rotted, some have sprouted, but none seem to have moved far from where the heavy fruits fell. The spreading limbs have cast a dark green shadow of seedlings on the forest floor, short whips growing too close to the coarsely fissured gray trunk ever to bear fruit of their own.

The largest avocado trees in this stand, their trunks 60 feet high and 2 feet in diameter, were probably planted in the early years of Brazilian independence. At the time, this land on the southern bank of the Rio Ayayá, a tributary of the Amazon, belonged to the Baron of Santarem, who in 1825 built a forty-room *palacio* at the river's edge. With the labor of three hundred slaves, the forest was cleared for tobacco, sugarcane, and cacao. But slave traffic was banned in 1850, and even the possession of slaves was made illegal in 1888. In a few years, the forest had reclaimed the plantation.

Although other tropical trees now crowd in around them, the avocado trees have not been forgotten. There is still a narrow trail that follows the old oxcart track, and in season, the feet of José Ceriaco and others who live nearby keep the mud freshly churned. Because the lowest branch is well over his head, Ceriaco strips a length of bark from a cacao shoot and hobbles his feet, binding his ankles so that they are about eight inches apart. Then, embracing the avocado trunk with his arms and with the splayed soles of his bare feet, he hitches himself up the tree like an inchworm. Within moments he is standing safely on a major limb, reaching for avocados and throwing them down to his son, who loads the fruit into a palm-frond basket. Half a bushel later, Ceriaco descends, shoulders his load, and the two of them head back toward the river single file.

Much of the weight in Ceriaco's basket is avocado pit. Dominating the center of every avocado is a single spherical seed, 1½ to 2 inches in diameter, consisting of two large, fleshy cotyledons embracing a small embryo. A big pit is an advantage for a tropical tree if it will be germinating on the shady forest floor. The nutrients stored in the cotyledons will feed the seedling for weeks or months. But once this inheritance is exhausted, the seedling is on its own. Its survival will depend on whether or not the pit found transport. Those pits that remain where they fall might as well not germinate, for there are no competitors in the forest more overwhelming than one's parents.

When it comes to getting away, big pits are a handicap. A quarter-pound seed isn't going to be blown about by anything less than a hurricane, and in water an avocado pit sinks. Yet the fat seeds of *Persea americana* do get around—with the help of a fat fruit.

Spherical, oblong, or pear-shaped, avocados come in many colors: chartreuse, green, rust, maroon, purple, black. Skins may be papery or leathery or woody, and of different thicknesses. But inside every avocado is bright yellow flesh tinged with green and liberally supplied with oil, oil that makes the avocado the richest of all fruits, averaging a thousand calories per pound. This oil, which may account for up to 30 percent of the avocado's wet weight, is a staggering investment on the part of the parent tree, for synthesizing oil takes half again as much energy as synthesizing an equal amount of sugar. Yet as costly as it may be, the oil is what makes the avocado so good to eat.

"Four or five tortillas, an avocado, and a cup of coffee —this is a good meal," say the Guatemalan Indians. The saying is an old one. Avocados probably originated somewhere in southern Mexico or Guatemala. Exactly where is problematic; wild avocados have never been found. In 1916, the most primitive avocado that Wilson Popenoe, agricultural explorer for the USDA's Office of Foreign Seed and Plant Introduction, could locate was in the Verapaz Mountains of northern Guatemala—a lime-sized fruit with a thin layer of oily, fibrous flesh covering a seed that was nearly as large as the pits of avocados sold in supermarkets today.

Even such skinny fruits must have had enough fat on them to make them attractive, attractive enough to take home. When the avocados had been eaten, their pits were thrown out into courtyards, where some sprouted. The best avocados in the next generation were the ones traded or sold, the avocados most likely to become trees in other courtyards.

Century by century, casual selection improved the avocado, until some of the fruits weighed three pounds. By the time of Columbus all three horticultural races of avocados—the Mexican, Guatemalan, and West Indian—were well established.

Since then avocado culture has spread to every country possessing the tropical or subtropical climate that the trees require. In total tonnage produced, avocados now rank fourteenth among fruit—right behind apricots, strawberries, and papayas—and they are closing fast. Every greengrocer on Broadway has them stacked under awnings, and New Yorkers heading home six abreast along the concrete sidewalk stop to pick out the softest and the heaviest, dropping them into plastic bags. In Brazil avocados are dessert fruits; Ceriaco and his family first fill the seed cavity with sugar. In the United States, however, where indulgence in this fat fruit is perversely promoted as a way to stay thin, avocados are served earlier in the meal. Some are mashed with tomato, onion, and chile peppers to make guacamole, or pureed with sour cream, sweet cream, and chicken broth to make cold avocado soup. Others are simply cut in half and filled with cooked lobster or crabmeat.

Outside of California and Florida, seedling avocados stand no chance of surviving the winter, but the farther north one goes the more likely one is to find avocado pits saved, impaled on three toothpicks, suspended right-side-up in a tumbler of water, and left to germinate safely on the kitchen windowsill.

As effective as humans have been at moving avocado pits around, they are not the animal that avocado trees had in mind when they evolved the big pit. After all, humans are only recent immigrants to the New World, having crossed the Bering Strait a few tens of thousands of years ago. But if man was not the first animal to seek out these delicious fruits with their oversize seeds, what was?

In theory a fruit-eating animal is after the fruit, not the seeds, accidentally ingesting the latter while it feeds. Once inside the animal, the seeds are carried some distance before they are regurgitated or defecated. Some of the avocados in Ceriaco's basket have been nibbled, but judging from the tooth marks, none of the animals were capable of carrying an avocado very far, let alone swallowing the pit.

What Central American animal is capable of accidentally swallowing golf balls, and excreting them with impunity? The answer may be none of them, at least none that are extant, for the tapir is currently the only large animal in Central America. But in the Pleistocene, a geologic epoch extending from one million to ten thousand years ago, it was another matter. Paleontologists point out that then there were once as many different large animals in Central America as there are in Africa today.

South America's sixty million years of isolation while the Isthmus of Panama was submerged saw the evolution of several animals with the appetite and bulk needed to disperse avocados. Giant ground sloths, looking like a cross between a bear and a kangaroo, stood upright on a tripod created by their massive hind legs and thick tail. From this position they fed on treetops, pulling down branches with their long-clawed front feet. The largest, *Eremotherium*, weighed 5 tons and stood 16 feet high, as high as the tallest giraffe. Another Pleistocene browser was the large, loose-jointed *Macrauchenia*, a camellike beast that was a forerunner of the guanaco.

While either of these animals could have eaten avocados straight from the tree, it seems more likely that they preferred avocados on the ground, for only after the avocado is separated from the tree does the flesh soften to a buttery consistency. As long as the fruit remains aloft it stays hard.

Grounded avocados could have been eaten by *Toxodon*, a rhinoceros-size animal (without the horn) that was probably semiaquatic. Or they might have been eaten by glyptodonts. Glyptodonts, weighing a ton or more, had a domed carapace, an armored tail heavy enough to counterbalance the body as it moved and an armored head that could be withdrawn into the shell. These giant mammalian tortoises, rooting around in slimy avocado pits, could easily have swallowed a great many. So too could have gomphotheres, elephantlike beasts with tusks in both jaws. Or mammoths.

Which of these was the real avocado enthusiast must remain a mystery. The last survivors died out about nine thousand years ago, victims of competition from North American species, or overspecialization, or changes in climate, or the weapons of early man. Until someone finds fossil avocado pits in the remains of giant sloths or glyptodonts, their role in the avocado tree's evolution can't be determined. All that we can say, looking at the avocado pit, is that whatever swallowed it must have been big. As big as those fossil skeletons staring out at us from behind the dusty glass of museum cases.

With the extinction of the large animals in Central

America, it is a wonder that the avocado trees didn't become extinct as well. Might they have been rescued by early man? We can imagine some primitive hunter-gatherer picking up fallen avocados. He moves quickly, glancing fearfully over his shoulder, listening for the slightest noise. He has heard that this tree is where dragons come. But he can relax now; the dragons are gone. The riches of the avocado are all his—and have been ever since.

3

WHITE
BLOOMERS

January is catalog season. Bundles of color from seed companies and nurseries fall through the mail slot and drift up against the radiator in the front hall, a welcome change from the snow and sand and salt that tracks through the doorway. Each catalog announces something new, seldom anything totally new, but sufficiently different to attract attention. There is, I see, a new cultivar of *Dicentra spectabilis*, the bleeding heart. The pink, heart-shaped flowers of this perennial are so common that even in yards without a garden there is often one growing on the shady side of the house, its foliage hiding the end of a downspout. What is different about this new cultivar is the flowers: they aren't pink, they're white. The catalog has a glossy photograph to prove it, and the accompanying text explains that the shape of the flowers and their "pure, starch-white cleanness" are reminiscent of turn-of-the-century bloomers. Not content to stop there, the catalog calls the plant 'Pantaloons'.

Underwear in the perennial border? "Underwear should be clean, not seen" I can hear someone saying. But at a time when you can see camisoles on the sidewalk, it's probably only natural to expect a little lacy lingerie among the lilies. Sales of 'Pantaloons' will be brisk, for there is nothing that excites some gardeners more than the sudden appearance of a white blossom instead of a colored one.

Will C. Curtis collected albino wild flowers. In his Garden in the Woods in Framingham, Massachusetts, now the headquarters of the New England Wild Flower Society, there were once eighty-two species, plants that Curtis discovered by himself in the wild or was given by friends who shared his pale passion. The white-flowered list begins with *Aquilegia caerulea*, a columbine whose flowers are normally blue, and ends with *Viola pedata*, the bird's-foot violet, whose upper petals should be a dark violet, the lower ones a deep lilac. In between are other white-flowered anomalies, some of which are now commercially available, others which are as rare as when Curtis found them. The contradiction in terms of a white cardinal flower, a white red bud, a white bluet, a white blue flag, or a white blue-eyed grass only adds to the attractiveness of these oddities. Curtis even had a few white-fruited specimens—a white chokecherry and a white low-bush blueberry. But his specialty was white bloomers— a white rose-shell azalea, a white purple trillium, a white wild pink. Some of these were collected from the wild, a practice that today is roundly condemned by conservationists. David Longland, current horticulturist at the Garden in the Woods and curator of the albino collection, wants to remind everyone of that. But upon discovering one of these white-flowered mutants growing on its own, gardeners even today will be tempted to dig it up and take it with them. The white-flowered specimen of *Cypripedium reginae*, the showy lady's slipper, that was transplanted from a sphagnum bog in western New York State to the Garden in the Woods in the 1930s has since been stolen, further proof of the covetousness that these white flowers inspire.

The white color in these flowers is caused not by a white pigment, but by tiny air pockets in the intercellular spaces of the petals that scatter light. When the normal pigments are absent, this scattering produces the ghostly pallor. The normal blue of cornflowers and the red of geraniums are caused by pigments called anthocyanins, the yellow of dandelions by ones called carotenoids. The synthesis of these pigments is genetically controlled, and in the case of 'Pantaloons' or any other white-flowered variant it is easiest to say that a genetic injunction has been issued, blocking the normal synthesis. Not only are the blossoms deprived of pigment, but the entire plant is as well. Examine the stems of white roses or snapdragons and you will see that they are a different color from the stems of red-flowered ones.

The necessary genes for blocking pigment synthesis are already present in some species. Among these plants, white-flowered offspring may appear as a result of normal cross-pollination. In other species, however, white-flowered plants are infinitely rarer because whiteness depends on a spontaneous mutation, perhaps an unpredictable cosmic ray slamming into a chromosome in just the right way.

How easily the white-flowered plants that do occur can

be propagated depends in part on whether this can be done vegetatively or whether it must be done by seed. 'Pantaloons' can be readily divided and stocks quickly increased, but if seeds must be produced, it is a different story. Crossing two white-flowered plants doesn't necessarily produce white-flowered seedlings. In many cases, the result is a noxious array of magentas.

The most publicized attempt to develop a strain of seeds that would grow into white-flowered plants has been David Burpee's search for a white marigold. The breeding began in 1920, but it was an announcement in the 1954 Burpee Seed Catalog that brought the subject to the public's attention:

> Burpee will gladly pay $10,000 in cash to the person from whom we first receive seeds that produce pure white marigolds as big as Man-in-the-Moon and as white as Burpee's Giant Fluffy White Aster or Snow-storm Petunia, as determined by a committee composed of the president of W. Atlee Burpee Co. and two other distinguished horticulturists. The decision of the majority of this committee shall be final.

On the same page of the catalog Burpee offered, for twenty-five cents, a packet of 'Man-in-the-Moon' marigold seeds, the nearest to a white marigold that Burpee's own breeding program had so far been able to produce. Thousands of gardeners took up the challenge, buying the seeds, selecting the whitest flowers, and mailing seed back to Burpee. The offer was renewed in each new edition of the catalog. Size became specified as "2½ inches or more across" and the close-to-white seeds that Burpee sold customers kept changing. In 1965 the most promising was called 'Hopeful'.

Finally, in 1975, the catalog carried an announcement that the contest was closed, and on Thursday, August 28, that same year, at Fordhook Farm near Doylestown, Pennsylvania, David Burpee handed a $10,000 check to Mrs. Alice Vonk of Sully, Iowa.

The news was in every paper. Alice Vonk became a celebrity. She may have begun with 'Man-in-the-Moon'; now she was as famous as the man on the moon. An amateur gardener had done what no giant corporation could do. In the excitement, writers forgot to mention that Burpee had kept up their own breeding program all along, and that the seeds they mailed out every year produced plants with whiter blooms than the year before. The truth is that when David Burpee paid Alice Vonk the $10,000, the company already had on hand a better white marigold than the one they paid her for. But David Burpee had said he would pay $10,000 for a white marigold, and he was true to his word. In the end the contest brought so much attention to marigolds that it was worth the price, even if Alice Vonk's seeds may not have been. In 1981, Burpee offered the first-named cultivar of white marigold, 'Snowbird', and gave a packet away with every $10 order. Since then, gardeners wanting white marigold seeds have had to pay.

"White," says Marc Cathey, "is the most common objective in flower breeding." The new director of the National Arboretum, Cathey speaks with authority, having just spent a year in the Kiplinger Chair in Floriculture at Ohio State University. "The alternative to any color is white. In landscaping, white is a major bridging plant. It smooths over clashing colors. Of course this can get to be a problem, too, because at dusk the white flowers become most conspicuous, and gardens that have too many such bridges become spotty in the evening." Cathey mentions the difficulties of producing a white flower. Even though a chrysanthemum is genetically white, the use of growth retardants may turn the blossoms yellowish, and cool temperatures may turn them pink. "Of course," he adds, "if you want the longest-lasting white flower, don't breed for white petals. Breed for white sepals or white bracts because they last longer. That's the secret to white hydrangeas and white poinsettias."

White impatiens growing in the shade, white phlox at the back of a border, white nicotiana at night, all of these are reasons to buy white-flowered plants. But perhaps the most important reason is that you know what you are getting. A catalog description that promises scarlet may deliver orange. There is much less room for confusion or subterfuge in the color white, and breeders keep looking for a white day lily, a white calceolaria, a white tetraploid geranium.

Given all the energy being devoted to developing white-flowered forms of those plants and the popularity of the introductions when they appear, one might expect white to be a popular color in the garden. In fact, it is not. The most popular color is red, by a long shot. A typical order of geranium seed from Ball Seed Company, in Chicago, is 60 percent red, 20 percent salmon, 7 percent bicolor, 7 percent white, and 6 percent pink.

What is wrong with the color white? For one thing, it gets dirty. Alan Arrowsmith, the executive vice-president of Pan-American Seed Company, remembers that in England white-flowered cultivars were much more popular in the countryside than in heavily industrialized cities like Sheffield.

At Pan-American, whites account for only 5 to 20 percent of sales, depending on the flower involved. Only in petunias do red and white sell neck and neck.

Color aside, perhaps the most common fault attributed to white-flowered cultivars is that they are less vigorous than their colored siblings—less vigorous, less hardy, less floriferous, less resistant to pollution and drought. Some claim that the popularity of moon gardens, in which all the plants are white, derived from the knowledge that any gardener who could keep such a garden looking good was a highly skilled horticulturist. But in many cases the criticisms of white bloomers are unfounded. White petunias are as vigorous or more so than any other color. Yet in other instances, such as the white bleeding heart, the prejudice is based on fact.

Despite the possible disadvantages, some people will rush to obtain any new white-flowered cultivar. They do so not because the flower is white but because the white is unusual. People will plant 'Pantaloons' not to commemorate some fraternity escapade in their past, but because if they hurry they will have a white-flowered plant when everyone else on the block still has pink. White-flowered cultivars may always be less widely grown than other colors, but like Tom Sawyer's whitewash, the more difficult they are to obtain the greater the demand. The most dramatic example is *Phalaenopsis violacea* 'Alba'. The flowers of this orchid are normally a blend of green and rose and magenta with a magenta purple lip, but occasionally, just occasionally, in centers of commercial orchid culture like Singapore, a white-flowered individual appears. The rarity of the event combined with the fact that *Phalaenopsis* plants can't be divided makes these most valuable. Ordinarily a plant of this species sells for $10 to $15, but an 'Alba' of fine quality may sell, usually privately, for $10,000 to $15,000.

In Crested Butte, Colorado, the meadows near the Rocky Mountain Biological Laboratory are filled with *Delphinium nelsonii*, a native species of larkspur. Of every thousand plants, 999 have flowers that are a normal deep blue, but one plant has pale or white ones. The discovery of one of these albinos is enough to send most people off in search of a shovel, but because of their proximity to the biological laboratory these particular albinos attracted the attention of two ecologists, Nickolas Waser and Mary Price. Ecologists like to observe flowers in their native habitat, rather than in the cosmopolitan crossroads of a suburban garden. For the last five years these two have been trying to explain why, given that they exist at all, these particular albinos are so rare in nature. What they have found is that *Delphinium nelsonii* is pollinated principally by the broadtailed hummingbird (*Selasphorus platycercus*) and several species of bumblebee queens. These pollinators, they discovered, don't visit the albino plants as often as they visit the normal blue ones. In fact, there is a 24 percent reduction in the number of visits if the flowers are not the normal blue. This reduction in visitation closely matches an observed 20 percent fewer seeds produced by the albinos. Thus, in spite of recurrent spontaneous mutations, the number of albinos doesn't increase because the pollinators are discriminating against them. It is analogous to a marigold breeder not bothering to fertilize the plants whose flowers have a washed-out appearance.

Why the hummingbirds and the bumblebees don't like

the white flowers isn't clear, and they aren't talking. The best guess is that they have trouble getting the nectar out of the albino ones. There is just as much nectar present, but without a white center on a blue background to serve as a target, the pollinators may have a harder time finding it. The data show that "handling times" for both hummingbirds and bumblebees are longer on white flowers than on blue ones.

There is disagreement as to whether bees have a preferred color. Hummingbirds apparently do not. But all pollinators are accustomed to receiving certain signals from a flower. In nature, flower colors are not casual choices, to be changed next season when hemlines drop and the demand for fins on automobiles returns. The color of a species' flower is the result of a long co-evolution between plant and pollinator, the latter learning to recognize the color as a signal that nectar and pollen are present, the former relying on consistent visits to fertilize the seeds. In a world where accurate communication is necessary for the survival of both parties, it is no wonder that pollinators choose to ignore a plant that gets its signals mixed.

The discovery that in at least one instance pollinators are avoiding the rare white-flowered plant raises the possibility that we human plant breeders are working at cross-purposes. While we are busy searching for novelty, the insects, who are a much more powerful guild of plant breeders, may be actively repressing it. We want to find a white-flowered mutant to decorate catalogs and gardens, and the bees and the hummingbirds may be seeing to it that we won't.

My own attitude toward these fair flowers is solidly ambivalent. On the one hand, they are gorgeous, and the delicacy of their appearance is often belied by a powerful scent. White flowers would be first on my catalog order if it weren't for their names. In an attempt to emphasize the unusualness of the white-flowered cultivar, plantsmen have come up with an eccentric assortment of names. I don't mind 'White Magic' or 'Ivory Tower', but I shudder at 'Snowflake', 'Carpet of Snow', 'Snowdrift', 'Ice Queen', and 'Glacier'. Don't the companies realize that their catalogs come out in January? No matter how unusual or how delightful these white bloomers may be, their names leave me cold.

4

NORTHERN COMFORT

The anxious barely weather winter, flinching at each forecast, fearful that the snow will be as deep as predicted. What if the oil burner quits? What if the pipes freeze? What if the roof collapses? The 11 P.M. news can fuel an all-night worry.

I have stopped following the forecast except to note that one does as well expecting the opposite. Our New England weather is so ill-behaved that storms arrive unannounced or cancel at the last moment. Skiers oscillate between ecstasy and grief. No one can be at ease for long with the mercury leaping up every so often or dropping out of sight. In short, the trouble with winter is that it is so disorderly.

Where I live, most of the houses are surrounded by

evergreens—arborvitae, laurel, rhododendrons, yew. The older the foundation, the bigger the bushes until they hide the porch, obscure the front walk, and brush against the windows of the second floor. This landscaping was designed for year-round effect, but it is now that we notice the evergreens, when the lilac, mock-orange, and flowering crabapple are bare. And it is now that we need them. Amid the hubbub of sudden thaws and unanticipated blizzards we need to have something that is not about to change, something to which we can turn to calm ourselves. Under the boughs of pine and hemlock, beneath junipers, behind boxwood, the short-range forecast is always shades of chartreuse, olive, jade, emerald, glaucous, viridian, or mignonette. We rally against winter under green banners.

Though people depend on evergreens for moral support, most don't know much about them. Asked to name a representative sample, they come up with a list of trees with needles—the familiar pines and spruces. Pressed for a broader example, they remember holly. We are all limited by what we see outdoors. These plants that help us through winter are the ones that have held onto their leaves despite the weather. They are actually a rather odd lot. Some that looked evergreen weren't and others that looked deciduous at first glance held onto their leaves: the needles of the larches all fell off, the broad leaves of leucothoe did not.

Evergreens are trees and shrubs that are green year-round, retaining their leaves for twelve months. We may not recognize them as such, but orange trees, date palms, and red mangroves are as evergreen as hemlocks and yews. Deciduous plants, on the other hand, are ones that lose their leaves for part of the year, becoming bare. The falling foliage usually precedes an extended period of bad weather, in our case, winter. Let those who go to Florida from December to March wax eloquent about the beauties of autumn, with all the leaves turning color and dropping off. Those of us who have to stay behind and shovel snow look at a sugar maple turning orange and see a prophecy of doom.

We may never know why some leaves are evergreen and others deciduous. There are likely to be several reasons in each case. But we do know a little about the tradeoffs, the difference between a leaf that lasts one summer, and one that lives much longer.

Every leaf is essentially a site for photosynthesis, and that site may be thought of as a solar-powered factory where carbohydrates are assembled out of carbon dioxide and water, using sunlight as an energy source. Whenever a new leaf grows, the plant must draw on its resources to build the factory. At the very least, the leaf has to be kept on the plant until it has returned resources of equivalent value.

Evergreen leaves and deciduous leaves differ in their costs of construction and the rates at which they can photosynthesize. The leaves we rake off the lawn every fall were inexpensive to build and capable of fast photosynthesis. By fall, they had more than paid back their cost. Because keeping them alive during the winter would have cost more than growing new ones next spring, they were shed.

The evergreen leaves that accompany us through winter, on the other hand, are more expensive to build and slow at photosynthesis. As a result, they take longer to pay back their costs. In addition, the leaves we see out the window now are constructed to carry loads of snow and ice without breaking, to survive freezing, and to resist drying out. What's more, they have been protected against insects and other enemies. These are more likely to discover and attack a long-lived leaf. All of this—the internal bracing, the oils and waxes, the insect repellents—add to the initial cost of a leaf. They not only add to its cost, some of them may reduce its efficiency. Slowing down the exit of water vapor to prevent desiccation, for example, also tends to slow down the entrance of carbon dioxide needed for photosynthesis.

It is impossible to say which is cause and effect: whether evergreen leaves live longer because it takes longer to make up for being expensive to build and inefficient at photosynthesis, or whether their expense and inefficiency are preparations for a long life.

Suffice it to say, the options for a leaf are the same as for Greek heroes—a short and glorious life, or a long and tranquil one. Neither choice is clearly superior, and evergreen and deciduous species live side by side all over the world. In northern Germany, careful studies have been made of the deciduous European beech and the evergreen Norway spruce. In the beech leaf, photosynthesis can proceed more than four times as fast as in the spruce needles. Stands of beech annually take up some 3.5 tons of carbon per acre in photosynthesis. Norway spruce trees, by virtue of their having at any given time four or more years' worth of needles photosynthesizing at once, and their photosynthesizing on warm winter days when the beech is leafless, do even better—6 tons of carbon per acre. If the spruce were as deciduous as the beech, its annual gain would be reduced to a mere 2 tons per acre.

Because they last all winter, there is a tendency for us to think that evergreen leaves are immortal. They aren't.

Some live only twelve months, scarcely qualifying as ever-greens. The so-called live oaks shading the antebellum mansions of the deep South remain green all winter but, in a flurry of spring housecleaning, drop all their old leaves when the new ones appear. The needles of white pine (*Pinus strobus*) turn brown and fall off at the end of their second summer. This is also the beginning of the end for mountain laurel foliage (*Kalmia latifolia*). For other familiar ever-greens, such as American holly (*Ilex opaca*), rosebay (*Rhododendron maximum*), and hemlock (*Tsuga canadensis*), three years is the limit. In general, conifer needles, like those of spruce and yew, live longer than the foliage of broadleaved evergreens: the needles of English yew (*Taxus baccata*) live six to ten years, of Sitka spruce (*Picea sitchensis*) nine to eleven.

Leaf life spans are not popularly recited, like batting averages, but for the record the longest-lived leaves are probably needles of *Pinus longaeva*, a pine that retains so many years' worth of needles that its branches resemble fox-tails. These trees, which are native to high elevations in the Great Basin of Utah, Nevada, and California, are closely related to both bristlecone pine (*P. aristata*) and foxtail pine (*P. balfouriana*). Recently, however, they have been separated as a distinct species. Their needles commonly persist for an unrivaled twenty-five to thirty years. One individual, growing in the Snake Range of White Pine County, Nevada, was found to have needles thirty-eight years old, still green and apparently still capable of photosynthesis.

There is an evergreen whose leaves seem to live even longer. *Welwitschia mirabilis* grows only in a strip of desert along the coasts of Namibia and Angola. The plant has a trunk that reaches 5 feet in diameter, but seldom exceeds a foot in height. From the top rise two leathery, straplike leaves 6 to 8 feet long. If they were intact, each leaf might measure 3 feet wide, but most leaves have torn into long strips, which in turn have twisted and curled. *Welwitschia* plants can live for a century and so do their leaves. At least, they give the appearance of lasting that long. But *Welwitschia* cheats. The leaves continue to grow indefinitely, new portions being added to the end attached to the plant, while the oldest portions die off at the other end.

Why don't evergreen leaves live forever? Some of them get shaded out by new leaves above them. Others get eaten. And some just get old. In both evergreens and deciduous leaves, there is a decline in photosynthetic efficiency with age. Evergreen conifer leaves are 30 to 50 percent less efficient with each passing year.

Plant physiologists are quick to point out that the life of a leaf is dependent on the needs of the plant as a whole. Some are adamant that there is no such thing as a fixed life span. There may not be, but northern winters cleanly separate foliage into two camps: those that are with us and those that are not.

Like bowerbirds—who build courtship structures of twigs and grass, decorated with colored fruits, petals, shells, buttons, bottle caps, and car keys—we are eclectic. Set on suiting ourselves, we have decorated our homes with evergreens chosen both from nearby and from other continents. The shrubbery that results is quite unnatural, but its purpose is to draw our attention away from the bare, lifeless limbs on the horizon.

There are parts of the country where the view out the window is naturally an evergreen landscape; I just don't happen to live in one. Where the soil is poor, for instance along the shore of the Great Lakes or in the Pine Barrens of New Jersey, evergreens often outnumber deciduous plants. Explanations for this include the possibility that nutrients are too scarce to sustain the high rate of photosynthesis that ordinarily occurs in deciduous leaves. Another possibility is that evergreens can retrieve more nutrients as their fallen leaves rot since they drop them over a longer period of time than deciduous plants do. Deciduous trees that lose their leaves just before they go dormant for winter are in the worst position to recover nutrients from them.

The winter-weary traveler who seeks solace in the virtually unlimited company of evergreens will have to fly either north or south. Few of us are eager to go north: the weather is bad enough here. The tropics, on the other hand, are a favorite destination. People head south in search of warmth and they find evergreens, although most aren't immediately recognized as such. Red and yellow hibiscus line the runway, coconuts surround the pool. With our northern conceptions of what evergreens are supposed to look like, these may not seem like evergreens. Along with the breadfruit and the banyan, they are taking advantage of the same thing that attracted the tourists—year-round sunbathing. The forest contains infinite shades of green, layer upon layer of evergreen leaves scrambling for the light.

Although most tropical trees are evergreens, here, too, there are deciduous species mixed in, now and then a bare crown amid the greenery. These plants drop their leaves not in response to cold but in response to a shortage of water. As one moves from uniformly moist regions to ones with a pronounced dry season, the percentage of deciduous species increases, until the forests during that dry season are as bare as temperate woods in midwinter. Cold is not the only reason to close up shop.

An extreme example, though not a tropical one, of leaves being lost because of dryness is *Fouqueria splendens*, the ocotillo or coach whip. A spiny shrub of the New Mexican desert, it is leafless most of the year; but when rain falls, it puts out short leafy branches. As soon as hot, dry weather returns, the leaves are shed. If weather permits, the ocotillo repeats this cycle several times a year.

Evolutionists speculate that the deciduous habit of plants first appeared in one of these dry-season environments, plants only secondarily moving into regions where the off season was cold rather than dry. Whatever their history, birches, maples, hickories, and elms are the rule in temperate forests, trees that drop everything in bad weather.

The increase in the proportion of deciduous species as one moves from tropics to the temperate zone reverses itself as one moves farther north still. If we were to head north we would encounter steadily more evergreens, of the sort we are familiar with—trees with slender, tough needles designed to withstand snow and ice. This switch from a deciduous-dominated to an evergreen-dominated forest as one moves into the boreal regions is another conundrum. Partly, it may be due to the extremely short season there for photosynthesis. When summer takes place, on one afternoon in July, there is probably simply not enough time for some deciduous leaves to pay back their cost. It may be that the plumbing of spruces and firs is particularly able to withstand the stress of freezing. It may also be true that some of the evergreens are using their leaves as warehouses to store nutrients needed for photosynthesis. This would permit them to begin photosynthesis even when nothing can be moved up out of the frozen roots. Deciduous species never disappear completely, but they become less and less numerous as one travels north, tending to grow close to the ground where temperatures are briefly the warmest.

Flying over a boreal forest this time of year, one sees mile after mile of black spruce, white spruce, balsam fir. Each a conical spire, they shed snow as swiftly as a slate roof. Their tiny needles are tough, and their branches are flexible. These are trees built for the worst of winter.

There really is no need to go north to see this. Every year, bits of boreal forest come to us. Tractor-trailers loaded with balsam fir, each tree carefully bundled, begin crossing the Canadian border as Americans are washing up from Thanksgiving dinner. The balsam fir is native as far south as the mountains of southwestern Virginia, but it flourishes in colder climes, growing north to the edge of the tundra. In Eastern Canada, balsam firs are grown on plantations, where the trees are pruned and fertilized. After ten to twelve years, a tree is 6 feet tall and ready to be shipped south.

Overnight, acres of greasy asphalt are transformed into fragrant groves. The aroma of needles crushed underfoot overwhelms every other smell. People pass from tree to tree, checking conformation, looking for the best. Having a tree is a Christmas tradition. The origins of the tradition, however, are obscure. The first decorated trees in America may have been those of Hessian mercenaries during the American Revolution.

What is most interesting about the Christmas tree tradition is not the decorations but the tree itself. What prompted Germans, centuries ago, to bring an evergreen indoors? I cannot help suspecting that the tree was intended to protect the household from winter, a talisman that would in time bring back summer.

It is an argument for our having not been so quick to throw out the tree when the holidays were over. If a couple of inches had been sawn off the butt of each tree when it was brought home, and the reservoir of the tree-holder kept filled, the balsam fir would be fresh and green even now.

This is not to say that the lights and ornaments should have been left on. They go with Christmas. But the balsam fir goes with winter. Some of the flat needles are eight years old. They have seen more bad weather than most of us can imagine. We might all be able to sleep better if we knew there was still a green tree downstairs, if we could crush a needle or two on the way to bed.

5

GUESTS AT WORK

Praise the large estate,
but cultivate a small one.
VERGIL

Unless severely pruned, small estates grow into large ones. The change is gradual, insidiously so, but the unmistakable proof is that each year there is more to do. Seduced by promises that sweet potatoes can be grown in the far North, we add them to a catalog order that is already longer than last year's, and then to make room the vegetable garden has to be enlarged once again. What began as space for six tomato plants comes to resemble a truck garden.

At the same time, perennial beds spring up like mushrooms. The house may already be surrounded, yet who can resist a bargain collection of day lilies? Small matter that planting fifty unnamed seedlings means plowing up yet another chunk of the back lawn. You say it will mean less grass to cut, but this isn't true when with each mowing the edge of the meadow recedes, and a new strip of lawn appears.

Everywhere the landscape becomes punctuated with new responsibilities: grapevines that need pruning, asparagus beds that need weeding, bird feeders that need filling. And yet the expansion continues, spurred on by both success and failure. If the strawberry harvest is poor, you are tempted to try raspberries. If the strawberries do well, you double the planting. Then there are the long-range plans that sneak up on you: today's idle dreams about water lilies, brick patios, and sheep have a way of becoming tomorrow's realities. In short, the virtues of smallness are academic, for smallness is next to impossible.

When in the course of events the small estate has become too large to be cared for by the residents alone, it is time to consider guests. The guests, of course, have been around ever since you acquired a place in the country, but until now they have been visitors. Putting them to work should be easy. It is, after all, what they said they wanted to do when they invited themselves to visit. However, there are limits to what guests like to do.

Guests like to work outdoors, provided the weather isn't rainy, snowy, cold, dark, or buggy. They would rather reap than sow, and they are adept at ignoring weeds. If there is a choice between doing something by hand or with a machine, the machine is a clear favorite. In general, the bigger and noisier the project, the more eager guests are to help. I'm periodically sorry that there aren't more uses for dynamite.

On the other hand, do not let their limitations prevent you from using guests to the full extent of their enthusiasms. When there is work to be done, and every extra cent is being spent on seed, fertilizer, and gasoline, free assistance isn't something to disregard. Large estates can be maintained with help from guests, provided you accommodate them somewhat. In my case, I built them a sugarhouse.

As soon as I let it be generally known that I was going to make my own maple syrup, guests started showing up to help, talking of sugar on snow. What few of them realized, and all soon learned, was that it takes an enormously long time to reduce 35 gallons of sap to 1 gallon of maple syrup—so much time that the boiling must continue into the night. In New Hampshire, March nights are always cold and dark, and often rainy or snowy. I was boiling the sap outdoors in the driveway and at night the guests congregated indoors. Because they wouldn't come out, I had to move in.

When Noel Perrin built his sugarhouse in Thetford, Vermont, he made it eight by eleven feet, large enough to house his Lightning evaporator, but a bit cramped for guests. I decided on ten by twelve feet, calculating that the 36-percent extra floor space would accommodate a few armchairs to one side. I also decided to make a post-and-beam sugarhouse, the result of an infatuation with tusk tenons and housed dovetails that I'd contracted from Ted Benson's *Building the Timber Frame House*. I happened to have a score of six-by-sixes and a few eight-by-eights. These had come from our own white pines, enthusiastically felled by guests and almost as eagerly squared with a chain saw. After a couple of years in the barn, they had dried nicely, but none were longer than 12 feet; hence the maximum dimensions of the sugarhouse.

Elisabeth and I spent a month and a half chiseling out mortises and shaping tenons, an experience that instilled a lasting reverence for nails, lag screws, and angle irons. In the end we had a pile of irregularly notched timbers ready for a raising. To raise a 50-by-100-foot barn takes 300 people equipped with long pike poles. Our little sugarhouse was almost too easy. We dispensed with pike poles and raised it in an hour with a pair of guests. When all the oak pins had been driven in and a tiny pine tree stood on the topmost rafter, we paused to celebrate and plan the next step.

It would have been simplest to sheath the sugarhouse in boards, like any other shed, but as I was building the sugarhouse for guests, I fancied it up a bit. I won't say I overdid it, but I admit that I probably have the only sugarhouse on the continent with a bay window—complete with diamond lights and a window seat. I didn't have to buy the bay window; I rescued it from a building about to be bulldozed, kept the pieces in the barn for five years, and spent a week trying to figure out how to reassemble them. I put as much glass into the sugarhouse as possible, partly because I like sunlight, and partly because discarded storm windows are cheaper than rough pine boards at twenty-five cents a board foot. I even used a pair of salvaged greenhouse vents for steam vents. Two by eight feet, with cypress frames, these were so large that what should have been a small cupola became a clerestory extending two-thirds the length of the building. When I saw how the light came in through the high windows, I knew that the sugarhouse would be a major attraction.

I'm always ready to start tapping the trees on February 5, my birthday, even though I know I should wait for Washington's. Last year Elisabeth restrained me until the twenty-fifth, a rainy Wednesday, when, with more dedication than any postman, I waded through the wet snow with a brace and bit, drilling 2½-inch holes in the sugar maples, hammering in galvanized spiles, and hanging my seamless aluminum buckets.

I told Elisabeth I was only going to hang ten buckets, but the sap was already running so well that I ended up hanging all fifty. By the time I'd finished, the first buckets had an inch or two of cold, clear sap in them, and by Saturday we had collected more than a hundred gallons.

About seven o'clock that morning I fired up the evaporator with a mixture of dry pine and apprehension. Not only was the sugarhouse new, but I'd changed the evaporator design once again. Homemade evaporators may not be as efficient as commercial models whose pans have fluted bottoms, but as the typical homemade evaporator consists of a large, flat pan sitting on a pile of concrete blocks and bricks, it's easy to change the design in an annual effort to build the best flat-pan evaporator yet. The two-by-three-foot aluminum pan was the same (the $29 that this pan cost me compares favorably with the $705 cost of the smallest Lightning evaporator), but this time I'd installed a grate, a series of baffles to deflect the flames evenly, and a proper door. The secondhand grate I bought for $4—another instance of the kind of fiscal conservatism needed to prevent maple syruping from becoming a cash-flow chasm. I found the door in the woods. Long before there were sanitary landfills (town dumps), every farmhouse had its own. Ours contains the remains of several wood stoves and a couple of wood furnaces. It's only a matter of digging around in the club mosses and lady's slippers to find a door that fits.

Within a minute the fire was going, and I had to cut down the draft. A few minutes later small bubbles lined the pan, and scarcely had I added more wood before the entire pan broke into a rolling, foaming boil. A six-square-foot column of steam rose to the rafters, where it split and slid out the open steam vents. Comfortably seated in my own leather armchair, with a clear view out the windows, I was as proud as any engineer on a steam locomotive.

With a flat pan you have the option of making many small batches of syrup or one big one, acknowledging that the big one will be darker syrup because the sap has boiled longer. Early in the season, though, I've found that I can make one big batch of light amber, Grade A syrup. We added sap to the pan all weekend and fortunately ran out of sap just about the time that we ran out of weekend. Then it was only a matter of carefully boiling what remained in the pan until it was proper maple syrup. At the point that the syrup sheeted off a spoon there was still an inch in the pan— three gallons on the sugarhouse's maiden run.

We made 25 gallons that season, twice what we had any reason to expect from fifty taps. Some was Grade A, and some Grade B, which many people think tastes better anyhow. When the temperatures finally rose for good, and bacteria in the buckets began to make the sap cloudy, we made a massive 6-gallon batch of molasses-dark Grade C syrup which we use to sweeten baked beans.

The improvements in the evaporator and the walls that kept the cold north wind from blowing across the pan were partly responsible for the ease and speed with which we made syrup that year, but they were eclipsed by the help from the guests. People came to watch, and stayed to help. Passing cars slowed down and stopped. Neighbors who hadn't visited in a decade showed up. Every weekend station wagons disgorged whole families of city friends. With scarcely any prompting, they went to work. Some split wood, reducing cordwood to kindling, while others specialized in arranging the sticks in the fire so they would burn best. A couple of people stationed themselves over the pan, monitoring the sap level and slowly adding just enough to keep it steady. With a slotted spoon, someone else kept skimming off the foam, or mother, that forms on boiling sap. The guests kept this up all day, and what's more they did it at night. Outdoors it was 20 degrees Fahrenheit, but inside it was a moist 80. If you switched off the electric light, you could see the lower end of the smokestack glowing a cherry red.

More important than their help with the boiling, however, was their help with gathering sap. Most maple syrup producers now use plastic tubing, linking all their trees with a network of pipe that drains the sap from whole hillsides. The switch to tubing (which is expensive) has resulted in a lot of secondhand sap buckets (which are cheap). The aluminum ones I use came from Canada. They are conical and seamless, so if the sap freezes it doesn't do them any harm. They weigh about 20 pounds apiece when full. At the beginning of the season there is usually a foot or two of snow on the ground, crusted over just enough to bear your weight —except when you are carrying a full sap bucket. Then you break through every step of the way. A good run of sap, when the night has been well below freezing and the day is just a bit above, will fill most of the fifty buckets in a day, meaning that there is half a ton of liquid to be transported to the big blue storage barrels in the sugarhouse.

Guests, I find, are as good as any pipeline. Better, in fact, because they are self-cleaning. They don't wait for the buckets to be filled but fetch half-filled buckets, romping through the snow like golden retrievers. One eager but slightly bewildered guest asked if we did this year-round. Considering how many gallons of syrup we were making, I was sorry we didn't.

Yet to spend all your time counting the gallons or planning to expand next year is to overlook something even more special than homemade maple syrup. What is so unusual about guests at work is not only how much they accomplish but what a good time they have. The guests may be strangers. They are almost certainly of different ages and skills. And yet if the task is big enough—raising a barn, canning tomatoes, or bringing in a winter's firewood—they gladly work together. In a society that prides itself on labor-saving devices, most of us work alone, and tend to think of jobs in terms of solitary man-hours. Therefore, it is always a surprise to discover how much can be done by a group, whether it's carrying sap or shoveling sand, even if nobody is working his hardest.

What makes the work enjoyable is partly the good food laid out at meals, but it is also the freedom from cost accounting. Because no one is being paid, there is no need to ask if the compensation is adequate. The compensation is learning how to set a wedge or the best way to skin a tomato, and a share of pride in something big done well.

Anyone who thinks a work party is a contradiction in terms has never attended one. They are often held at large estates, and the public is invited. Here in New England, March work is maple syrup. When all the day's sap has been collected, we sit around in the new sugarhouse tasting the syrup's progress, dipping into the Sunday papers, and enjoying the sunlight that filters down through the rising steam.

6

SPRING TIME

From bed, up against an east-facing window, I can see the sunrise. For six months, the bed has doubled as an observatory, a four-posted Stonehenge, a feather-filled pyramid of Kukulcán in the Mayan city of Chichén Itzá. Here, clad only in a nightshirt and without even looking at the calendar, I can prove that this is spring, for the movement of the sunrise along the horizon is a precise indicator of the season.

Last December 21, the first day of winter, the winter solstice, when the day was shortest, the sun rose farthest to the south. It stayed there for several mornings, but then started back north along the horizon, playing hide-and-seek for a fortnight among the chimney pots and television fishbones on a distant roof before moving off through a tangle of bare branches. Morning after morning, the sun rose each day a little farther to the left until on March 20, the vernal equinox, the day I had been waiting for, the sun rose due east, directly over the center of the windowsill, and the shadows from the mullions fell straight across the bed. I proclaimed it spring.

Not quite three weeks later, of course, it snowed. Not just a few last flakes, but the worst storm of the winter, which closed the schools and buried the daffodils. "It's spring," I told a couple trying to push a Porsche out of a snowdrift. They didn't bother to answer. Like most people, they weren't sure that this was temporary, didn't know that deep snow is an excellent insulator, protecting buds and blossoms from the plummeting temperatures, and couldn't say that the biggest effect of the blizzard would be on the record books. But then, they didn't have the self-confidence that comes from months of astronomical observation.

The practice of archaeoastronomy—measuring seasons the way the ancients did—is more enjoyable if you cheat, if you understand that the movement of the sunrise is a result of the earth's axis of rotation being tipped 23.5 degrees from the vertical. This means that as the spinning planet makes its way around the sun, each hemisphere spends half the year tipped away. The snow and ice and freezing temperatures that result aren't caused by the sun's being farther away, but by the flatter angle with which sunlight is striking the earth —or, put another way, by the longer shadows of trees in winter. What sunlight isn't scattered or observed by the atmosphere is simply spread out too thin to keep us warm.

At the winter solstice, back on that darkest day of the year, the hemisphere we live in was tipped the farthest away from the sun, causing the sunrise to appear far to the south. Had I gotten out of bed and traveled to the Tropic of Capricorn (23.5 degrees south latitude), I would have cast no shadow at noon, the sun being directly overhead. Since then, the sun has been coming back. On the vernal equinox, it crossed the Equator at 5:56 P.M. Eastern standard time. On that date, day and night are equal, or so people think, but any latter-day archaeoastronomer with a watch can see that the day is longer than the night. Equal division of night and day actually occurred several days earlier—on March 17, St. Patrick's Day. The discrepancy between the astronomical equinox and the observed one is caused by atmospheric refraction that lifts the sun slightly at both sunrise and sunset, causing it to appear where it isn't.

Since the equinox, the sunrise has continued its progress toward its northernmost point, which it should reach on June 21, the summer solstice. On that day, the noontime sun will be directly over the Tropic of Cancer (23.5 degrees north latitude), and I will proclaim the first day of summer.

Without watching the sun to see when it rose due east, I might have missed the equinox, but I have other ways of telling that it is spring. Even with the shades drawn, it's hard not to notice that it has been getting lighter earlier. The difference, of course, is more pronounced the farther you are from the equator. At the equator, the days are always the same length, but here in the middle latitudes the time of the sunrise is as precise an indicator of the season as the sun's position on the horizon at dawn.

At Christmas in Boston, the sun wasn't rising until

7:12; yesterday morning, it rose at 4:50. The sun is also setting later, so there is twice the difference in additional day length. And by the time you have added the two periods of twilight, there is very little nighttime left. By now, after a particularly late night out on the town, it hardly seems worth going to bed since it will be light so soon. Some people, whose morning faces have acquired a permanent glaze, are saying nasty things about springtime. They mumble about moving their bed into a closet or reinstalling World War II blackout shutters.

Today, on the fourth Sunday of April, we get some relief. Sunrise was an hour late. This astronomical achievement, this gusset in the calendar, is a result of simply setting the clocks forward an hour at 2:00 A.M. Daylight Savings Time, as it is called, would have pleased Benjamin Franklin. While residing in Paris, he calculated that 64 million pounds of candles might be saved each year if Parisians would get up when the sun rose and conduct their business by daylight. He proposed a tax on windows with shutters and a firing of cannons in the streets to get people up and out at dawn.

The first serious proposal to reset the clocks came in 1907 from William Willett—an English builder, Member of Parliament, and a member of the Royal Astronomical Society—in a pamphlet entitled, "The Waste of Daylight." Succumbing to criticism, the notion languished until the Germans adopted Daylight Savings Time in 1916 to save fuel for the war effort. The United States soon followed, enacting and repealing various daylight savings plans for half a century until the Uniform Time Act of 1966 specified six months of daylight savings time from the last Sunday in April to the last Sunday in October. As is readily apparent, this period is not centered around the longest day in the year (at the end of June), but around the hottest day of the year (at the end of July). This anomaly has been brought to the attention of Congress, so far with no effect.

My eyesight is really too poor for me to be an astronomer. I can determine springtime all right, but the sun is the only star I can consistently find. But were I to go blind completely, I could still tell when it was spring. I could hear it announced, not by a radio or television commentator but by the dawn chorus of birds defending territories and attracting mates. Many of the birds in this springtime serenade are migrant pickers who have flown north to harvest a bumper crop of bird food to feed young mouths. A friend who tunes into "Morning Pro Musica," a program of classical recordings that opens with birdsong, has just reported that she was up and fully dressed hours early before she realized that the wake-up calls were the real things.

Many birds, especially insect eaters, fly south for the winter, either because food is scarce or because the winter days are simply too short to gather enough food to keep themselves warm during the night. In the summer, the situation is the reverse: lots of food and long days to gather it in. In June in Umiat, Alaska (69 degrees 23 minutes north latitude), where the sun is still above the horizon at midnight, robins have been seen feeding their young an average of 137 times a day. But the timing and coordination of migration in the temperate zones has to be precise, for the margin of error is small. Males who arrive too late may find all the best territories taken. Females who nest too early may lose their eggs to a cold snap. Insect eaters, like swallows, have such specialized bills and digestive systems that they cannot feed on seeds or other food even in an emergency. If they arrive before their food does, they starve.

Personally, it hasn't been easy learning to tell springtime, sitting up in bed every morning to practice. Therefore, I cannot help but be impressed that the red-winged blackbirds all know when to return to the cattail swamps or that the Canada geese know when to fly honking northward. Some birds migrate with deadline timing. The population of northern cliff swallows breeding in San Juan Capistrano manages to return to California within a few days of March 19 each year. Other people can set their calendars by the return of buzzards to Hinckley, Ohio, around March 15. The birds know that it is spring, but how?

One of the most studied migratory birds is the white-throated sparrow, the one that calls "Old Sam Peabody, Peabody, Peabody." Beginning in late February and March, the birds, which winter in the eastern United States, begin fattening up for the flight which will take them as far north as Canada. At the same time, hormones needed for reproduction are produced by the pituitary gland, and the birds' gonads begin to redevelop. By the time the birds reach their summer breeding grounds in May, they are ready to mate and lay eggs.

The timing of this portion of the reproductive cycle is regulated not by a calendar, an almanac, an observatory, the morning paper, or the evening news, but by a clock somewhere inside the bird's brain. This clock is capable not only of measuring time but of recording the duration of daylight. Anything less than nine hours of light a day will halt all fattening and gonad development in white-throated sparrows. With sixteen hours of light a day, these changes proceed the fastest.

The same change in day length, which is such a nuisance for humans trying to sleep late, is for birds the most important environmental timer. Day length is the essence of seasons. Provided you are not situated on the equator, cyclical changes in day length can be relied upon. One spring may be colder, wetter, drier, cloudier than another, but how often do people say, "The days have been shorter than last year"?

So powerful is day length in determining some birds' behavior that it can be experimentally used to override other natural signs. Juncos can be made ready to breed in the dead of winter, crows to fly north in the fall, indigo buntings to fly south in the spring. More practically, chicken farmers use electric lights to lengthen the days in midwinter to make their hens lay more eggs and gain weight faster. How the birds get this message isn't completely understood, but blind ducks respond to longer days with the same explosive growth of their testes as do sighted ones. The light goes directly through their skulls.

As early as the seventeenth century, Dutch bird netters knew that day length affected birds. Birds that they kept on a regimen of reduced light during the spring and summer, and then exposed to the long days of late summer, would sing as though it was spring. These birds were used as singing decoys to lure fall migrants into nets.

The first scientific report, however, of a biological response to the duration of light in a twenty-four-hour period (photoperiodism) involved not birds but plants. W. W. Garner and H. A. Allard, working for the United States

Department of Agriculture in Beltsville, Maryland, after World War I, were trying to get a mutant strain of tobacco called 'Maryland Mammoth' to flower. Unlike other tobacco, it remained vegetative (nonflowering) during the summer despite persistent efforts to make it bloom. Finally, on July 10, 1918, Allard placed three plants in a light-tight "doghouse" for seventeen hours each night, and the plants promptly flowered.

All plants have subsequently been shown to belong to one of three categories: long-day plants, which flower only if the day length is longer than a critical number of hours; short-day plants, which flower only if the day length is shorter than a critical number of hours, and day-neutral plants, which are unaffected by day length.

Long-day plants include red clover, black-eyed Susan, larkspur, radish, and dill, as well as sugar beet, rose of Sharon, and most winter wheat. If I were looking to the vegetable garden for proof of spring, I would look to the spinach. This long-day plant goes to seed, or bolts, not when it gets warm, as so many people think, but when the days get to be longer than thirteen hours (by which time it has often gotten warm). In addition to making certain plants bloom, long days are responsible for budbreak on European beeches, runners on strawberry plants, and bulbs on onions. One should be careful not to take as a sure sign of spring a plant parked under a streetlight.

There are still other ways I could determine spring from the natural calendar, all indirect ways of measuring the presence of long days. I could look to see if snowshoe rabbits and ermine had changed their coats from white to brown. I could watch for mares, raccoons, and minks to come into heat. They are, I'm told, stimulated by long days. If I were especially diligent, I could see whether young coho salmon were migrating to the sea or female aphids were giving birth to parthenogenetic young (which, in turn, can give birth without being fertilized). Some time, I intend just to stand quietly in the woods and listen for the sound of tons of antlers falling, shed from the heads of deer, elk, moose, and caribou. Sportsmen prefer their antlers firmly attached to the skull, so they shoot their quarry in the fall rather than wait until the spring, when antlers are free for the taking.

Since antlers take only four months to replace, regardless of their size, it is possible to make deer produce more than one pair a year, just as white-throated sparrows can be made to breed twice. Sika deer from Japan were placed in a light-tight barn in Massachusetts and subjected to two-, three-, and fourfold accelerations of the natural increases and decreases of day length. The results were new antlers every six, four, or three months. There was a limit, however. Those quick-change headpieces got progressively smaller, and a sixfold acceleration resulted in no antlers.

Even more surprising, however, was what happened to the deer when there was no change in day length at all. When some of these Sika deer were exposed to constant photoperiods—either eight, sixteen, or twenty-four hours of light a day—the deer continued to shed and replace their antlers, but not at the same time of year, nor once a year. Rather, they replaced their antlers an average of once every ten months.

Such a rhythm, which persists or "free-runs" in the absence of external cues, is called an endogenous rhythm.

Daily endogenous rhythms, called circadian ones, are well known. Jet lag is the result of tampering with our circadian rhythm of sleep. Annual ones—sometimes called circannual, because their period is approximately a year instead of approximately a day—are much less well known. This is partly because, to demonstrate their existence, experimenters must keep the organism in a constant environment for more than a year. Yet antler growth in deer and testes development in ducks have both been proved to be under endogenous control. One of the advantages of a circannual clock is that it can provide a reliable guide in situations where there are no temporal cues. A bird wintering near the Equator, where day and night are always equal, might not know it was time to start north if it did not have a clock inside that struck spring.

Even in such cases, temporal cues are still needed sometimes, to force the rhythm into a yearly one. Without this *Zeitgeber*, or time-giver, as the Germans call it, the circannual clocks would be off, causing seasonal events to occur more or less than once a year.

As seasonal rhythms are more closely examined, more of them will probably prove to be controlled from within. It is even likely that human beings have circannual clocks. The notion that we, too, are affected by the seasons goes back to Ecclesiastes:

> *To every thing there is a season,*
> *And a time to every purpose under*
> *the heaven:*
> *A time to be born, and a time*
> *to die. . . .*

And to this must be added a time for excreting 17-ketosteroid in one's urine. I confess I haven't been very attentive to my production of urinary 17-ketosteroid, which is a measure of my production of male sex hormones. The peak, last November, passed me right by. Nor am I terribly enthusiastic about the trough in my annual output, due sometime in May. What excites me is the possibility that I am sensitive to the seasons. I, too, may be responding to changes in day length, perhaps without even opening my eyes. My body may right now be undergoing profound changes as a direct result of longer days or in concert with some internal rhythm. If I could be sure of this, I would be spared another six months of searching for empirical signs of spring. I could stop sitting up at dawn to mark the position of the sunrise. I could stop timing day length. I could stop listening for the first birdcall. I could stop wondering if the caribou have shed their antlers. Instead, I could quite justifiably proclaim, "I feel like spring, and thus it is Spring."

7

CROWBARS, GLACIERS, AND ZEN TEMPLES

Shortly after income tax is due, New Hampshire gardeners begin brandishing their crowbars. Rearranging the rocks is a centuries-old tradition in the Granite State, where rocks may compose 50 percent or more of the soil volume. For some, the labor is a good way to dispel one's feelings about the federal government.

The high ground dries out first and is usually reserved for the earliest peas. All peas are poor yielders, but no crop, peas, or potatoes, can equal the annual harvest of fieldstones. Like gray seals in the sea of mud left by the melting snow, some of these gently rounded rocks surface each spring. Their companions rest beneath them, to be discovered only by a plowshare, the revolving tines of a tiller, or someone's spading fork.

Fieldstones between ¼ and 2½ inches in diameter are called pebbles by soil scientists. Those between 2½ and 10 inches are termed cobbles. Up to 24 inches in diameter, the specimen is a true stone. Anything larger is a boulder.

Most people don't even try to remove all the pebbles from the soil, for they fear that, like boning a sardine, there will be very little left. Those, however, who want all their carrots to be straight try to root out all the cobbles and stones within a foot of the surface, and those who are determined to have straight rows end up moving the boulders. For them, what the stone is called is less important than what it weighs. A cubic foot of granite weighs approximately 165 pounds; so does a sphere 15 inches in diameter (fieldstones are seldom cubic).

Cobbles are light enough to pick up, but they can be deceiving, flaring unexpectedly to stone proportions. Stones, in turn, too often prove to be boulders as you dig around them. In both cases it helps to try wiggling the candidate first to see if removing it will be the work of a moment or a morning. While most people have grown resigned to removing rocks, a few people actually seem to like the work: the bigger the boulder the better.

A logging chain and a pair of oxen were once used for pulling boulders. The same chains are in use today but hitched to the drawbars of tractors. Black powder has been replaced by dynamite for those courageous enough to use either one. And finally, there are bulldozers with rock-picking blades that in theory can rake out all the rocks but, unless the operator is especially skilled, tend to roll up the topsoil as well.

None of these technological advances, however, diminish the role of the crowbar, a tool that has remained virtually unchanged since the land was settled. The bars are now steel, not iron, but, with one end flattened to slip under the edges of things, they are just as long, straight, solid, and heavy as they ever were. When the year's fieldstone harvest begins, crowbars are the first tools out of the barn.

Properly used, a crowbar affords the mechanical advantage of a first-class lever. When supported by a fulcrum—usually a smaller stone placed beside the one to be moved—the product of the magnitude of one force and its lever arm (the distance between the force's point of application and the fulcrum) equals the magnitude of the other force and its lever arm. In other words, a 500-pound stone can be balanced by 100 pounds on the other end of a 6-foot crowbar, provided that the fulcrum is only one foot from the stone. This mathematics is courtesy of Archimedes, who is said to have boasted, "Give me a firm spot on which to stand, and I will move the earth." As anyone from New Hampshire knows, Archimedes didn't need a place to stand, he just needed a fulcrum on which to rest his crowbar. He could have—indeed should have—planned to stand on the end of the crowbar.

Once a rock has been unearthed, it has to go someplace. Small ones are piled into buckets and unceremoniously dumped on the nearest rock pile. Larger ones are loaded onto a stoneboat, which is then dragged to one of the old stone walls, walls that were built many generations ago to fence off cultivated land from adjacent pasture. When these walls were built, it was said that "a man and a pair can build a rod a day," but it is hard to imagine someone doing that now. Instead, the work takes all the hands that can be mustered. Amid shouts to watch one's fingers and much grinding of boulder upon boulder, the new ones are worked up on top of the old wall and chinked with small stones so that they are stable.

In New Hampshire, where it can frost eleven months of the year, residents have come to accept a degree of hardship. Most don't mind clearing land for planting. If they get upset, it's about having to move rocks from the same piece of ground year after year. The seemingly inexhaustible supply of rocks has been enough to drive some of them west.

Ask almost anyone where the rocks come from and you'll learn that the glacier brought them. The glacier did bring them, a massive ice sheet moving down from Canada grinding smooth the north sides of hills and mixing the fine particles with coarse stone torn from the south sides. Mixed together, the rock worn smooth from tumbling, the soil and stones were eventually deposited as glacial till. Some of the boulders can be traced to specific ledges of bedrock. Some have been moved hundreds of miles, but most only a few. Called glacial erratics, these rounded stones were the first solid ground the Pilgrims encountered—if in fact they stepped ashore onto Plymouth Rock.

The last glacier to cross New England, the source of most of the glacial till people try to garden in, was the Wisconsin Glacier. It left about fourteen thousand years ago, gone back, people quip, for more rocks. Hence the glacier can hardly be blamed for the reappearance of stones on the surface of cultivated land each spring.

The trouble is the "seed rocks," they say in Maine. Unless you take out all the pebbles, they will grow into stones. They are only half-joking. The stones aren't growing, but they are definitely coming up—gradually rising to the surface. Work the same ground for a decade and you will discover that a rock that was once too deep to worry about is, in a few years, closer to the surface. Trying to rake soil up over it is only a temporary measure; eventually it will have to be dug out.

This vertical movement of the fieldstones is not simply an artifact of soil erosion; it is the result of frost heaving. In the fall the soil freezes first beneath stones, because stones are a better conductor of heat than soil. Or, put another way, soil is a better insulator than rock. In a sea of insulation, stones are chilly islands.

Because most glacial till has a fairly high water content, ice forms beneath fieldstones when they freeze, and the expansion of this ice forces them upward. Even when the ice thaws, the stones do not return to their original positions because during thawing particles of soil seep into the cavity beneath, partially preventing the stones from dropping. Like a ratchet on a car jack, each freeze-thaw cycle gradually lifts the fieldstones toward the surface. In a very cold winter there may actually be two thrusts per freeze. Ice expands when it initially forms, but as the temperature plummets, the ice contracts. In the reverse process, when this very cold ice finally melts, it must expand a second time, pushing the stone once more.

In theory, the upward movement of fieldstones should result in pure soil, all the stones above the frost line having been pushed to the surface and carried away. What a vision! Acres of pure, deep soil, and crowbars rusting away unused. Alas, the fastest stones move only an inch or so a year, and most are orders of magnitude slower. Many millennia will pass before the rocks do, and before that the glacier will probably have returned with a fresh supply.

Against this prospect of an eternity of rock picking, it should be observed that there are those who like stony ground. "May the Emperor live until all the gravel has become moss-covered boulders," sing the Japanese in their national anthem. And not only do most Japanese gardens contain stones and boulders, but these have often been transported with care over great distances from mountains, rivers, and seashore. *Karesansui*, or dry landscape gardens, may consist of little except rocks.

Surrounded by the walls and buildings of a Zen temple on the outskirts of Kyoto, Ryōan-ji is a 30-by-78-foot rectangular expanse of coarse white sand raked into straight lines by an acolyte. Rising from the sand are fifteen rocks, arranged in five groups of five, two, three, two, and three rocks, respectively. Only fourteen, however, are visible. Regardless of where you stand to view the garden, one or the other of two small rocks is always hidden. Except for moss growing at the base of the rocks, there are no plants.

"Delivering over the Tiger Cubs" is the popular name for this dry landscape, and some see in the pattern of the rocks a mother tiger confronting a ferocious leopard as she ferries her two cubs across a stream. Others see a Confucian teaching: The virtue of a good ruler protects a country. Still others see Mount Shumisen, the resting place of Buddha, and the other eight mountains and eight seas of the Buddhist universe. But whether Ryōan-ji is one of the world's great masterpieces of religious art or a neatly tilled piece of bony land with 10 percent rock cover is a matter of perspective.

The components of Japanese rockwork are described by shape, not size. Each rock is assigned to one of five categories, categories borrowed from the five natural elements of the ancient Chinese—wood, fire, earth, gold, and water. The largest rocks to be moved weigh more than two tons, and there may well be 30 tons of total rockwork in a garden recreation of a mountain range (enough rock to build a New England stone wall approximately 3 feet high and broad, and 40 feet long).

Stone merchants who collect the stones in the first place are careful not to damage them, prying only on the backside or the bottom when digging them lest any of the moss and lichens growing on the face be scraped off. During transport cloth pads, straw mats, and scrap lumber keep rocks from banging into one another, a far cry from the rough passage rocks endure on a stoneboat. During especially long trips, some rocks are even sprinkled with water to keep the moss healthy.

The Japanese don't just pile rocks in a garden, they plant or root them, treating them as though they were trees or shrubs. Great holes are dug first, and enough of the rock, perhaps as much as two-thirds, is buried so that it looks like a natural outcrop. Rocks that look like they are afloat, detached from the earth, are deemed examples of unrefined placement.

Before soil is packed around the root of a rock, using the butt end of a pole, the rock is meticulously adjusted, a process made easier, in the case of the heaviest rocks, by hanging them from chains and a pulley attached to a tripod of logs. Wooden levers rather than metal crowbars are used because they are less likely to injure the rock's surface. Final alignment must accommodate the direction of the rock's ridges and lines, its so-called vigor. An old Japanese expression says that even the hearts of the coarse should not be forced. So, too, it is considered unforgivable to deprive a rock of its own natural beauty.

The subtleties of Japanese rockwork are largely lost on Westerners, in part because we prefer to move around in a garden rather than simply sit and contemplate it. This makes it hard to see a solitary rock as a mountain, an island, a celestial ship, or the seat of Buddha. For the Japanese, rocks will always have a special meaning that the rest of the world does not comprehend.

Yet Westerners can learn something from *karesansui*. Ryōan-ji dates from the sixteenth century. The rockwork in other gardens is even older. The oldest remains of any garden in Japan are a few rocks that were planted in the seventh century. Except for earthquakes, landslides, and the slight movements that result from freezing or root growth, there is little that nature can do to displace a rock. If they have been solidly placed, rocks will stay put for thousands of years. Moving a rock, even a short distance, may be a gardener's most lasting achievement.

New Englanders tend to view their spring rock picking as a chore to be gotten out of the way before they get down to the important parts of gardening. No one pays much attention to the rocks that have been moved. Instead, we concentrate on sowing annual crops, most of which, like corn, are incapable of reproducing themselves even once without human assistance. Herbaceous perennials are little better, dying out once their caretakers are gone. Compared to well-positioned rocks, even trees are short-lived, blowing down, burning up, or dying in a few centuries.

Japanese gardeners have capitalized on the constancy of rocks, their immutability. This is worth remembering when a big boulder must be dug out. We shouldn't curse the glacier that brought it or the ice that forced it to the surface, for to move a rock is to erect a monument. Proof of that can be found in Zen temple gardens. Or, closer to home, in the old stone walls deep in New Hampshire's woods.

8

GYPSY MOTHS

I may be accused of being soft on caterpillars, but gypsy moths are here to stay and we'd best learn to live with them. Gypsy moths have never been well received, and when their numbers increase, as they do periodically, people become alarmed and begin to talk about an end to the landscape as we know it. Throughout the Northeast this year, people have been getting up at town meetings and demanding to know what preventive measures are being taken, while privately they worry about property values going down.

I have been asked what I think of gypsy moths by people whose bumper stickers proclaim their love of four-legged animals. On occasion, they know, I have spoken enthusiastically of six-legged ones, and they wonder whether my enthusiasm extends to gypsy moths. They themselves, of course, are horrified—horrified by the thousands of dark, hairy caterpillars with their blue and red warts, horrified by the incessant leaf chewing, and revolted by the steady drizzle of caterpillar droppings from the branches overhead. Gypsy moths have aroused such enormous enmity that anyone even suggesting coexistence with them faces the modern equivalent of being ridden out of town on a rail. And yet the zeal with which some people call for their eradication provokes me to suggest just that.

Shortly after Patriots' Day, that celebration of the alarm spread by Paul Revere, William Dawes, and Samuel Prescott, a similar tocsin is sounded about gypsy moths. The morning papers begin to describe this year's infestation, calling the reader's attention to the silk tents in the crotches of cherry trees along the highway. The silk tents aren't built by gypsy moths, however. They are the nests of the eastern tent caterpillar, a native American insect that differs from the gypsy moth in both its construction of tents and its gregarious nature. At night, dozens of these caterpillars cluster together within each tent, venturing out by day to eat the leaves of wild cherry and apple trees. Although the tents are unsightly, tent caterpillars, with their white midstripe and rows of blue ovals, are seldom numerous enough to cause serious damage. Another caterpillar, the fall webworm, builds similar, but larger, tents late in the summer on the ends of branches. Within these tents, yellow green caterpillars feed. But since the leaves they are eating would have been shed shortly, their feeding does little damage to trees. Unlike the fall webworm or the tent caterpillar, gypsy moths do not make tents. But because tent caterpillar eggs hatch at about the same time as gypsy moth eggs, tent caterpillars are invariably victims of mistaken identity.

In late April or early May, or when the white flowers of the shadbush are open and the oak leaves are just beginning to unfurl, the eggs of *Lymantria dispar*, the gypsy moth, hatch. Although it was cold throughout the Northeast last winter, the mercury rarely reached the minus 25 degrees Fahrenheit needed to kill them. The newly emerged gypsy-moth caterpillars, buff-colored at birth, turn black in a few hours. They remain on the light brown, furry egg mass that is plastered to a tree trunk as long as the temperature is below 40 degrees Fahrenheit, or as long as it is raining. Then, with fair skies and warmer air, each tiny caterpillar, a mere eighth of an inch long, begins to ascend the tree on which it was born. As it travels, the young caterpillar lays down a trail of silk excreted by glands in its head. Reaching the topmost twig of the tree, the caterpillar keeps going, paying out the silken lifeline as it falls. Stopping abruptly in midair, the caterpillar begins to ascend the line, but before it regains that top twig, a breeze usually snaps the silk and the caterpillar—kept aloft by the length of silk and its own unusually long body hairs, which act as sails—is blown sidewise onto the branch of another tree. Here it climbs and falls once more until, after several such repetitions, the caterpillar settles down to feed hundreds of yards from where it hatched.

This ballooning is the gypsy moth's natural means of dispersal, the way it moves into new territory. Although most of the caterpillars being wafted about are not yet feeding, some people are already upset, irritated by skin rashes where the windblown caterpillars have bumped their bare arms. Others are bothered by having to pick caterpillars off the backs of their necks when they come in for lunch.

First-stage, or first-instar, larvae—as these caterpillars are called—chew small holes in the middle of leaves. After about a week of feeding, the larva stops, preparing to shed its skin. Twenty-four hours later, the skin suddenly ruptures behind the head and the caterpillar steps out of its old skin. It swings its body from side to side a few times, its long hairs straighten out, and in a few hours it begins to feed again. Second-instar larvae are larger and proportionately hungrier, and they begin to consume whole leaves, starting at the leaf's margin.

By the time the caterpillars have shed their skin twice more, at intervals of four to ten days, depending on temperature, and become fourth-instar larvae, their feeding behavior changes again. Instead of occasionally moving to the underside of a leaf or branch to rest, the caterpillars now travel down the trunk of the tree at dawn and spend the day hidden beneath a flap of bark, in a crevice in the trunk, or in some sheltered spot on the ground. At dusk, they climb to the foliage and resume feeding.

Two months after they have hatched, or about the first week in July, the caterpillars stop feeding for good. The largest caterpillars, resplendent with five pairs of blue spots followed by six pairs of red ones, are now as long as 2½ inches. The males have gone through five instars; the females, six. Both sexes have also gone through a lot of leaves. A late-instar caterpillar can convert 12 square inches of leaf into gypsy moth and gypsy moth droppings in twenty-four hours. The caterpillars have their preferences. Oak leaves are their favorite, but they will also eat leaves of apple, basswood, beech, gray birch, hawthorn, poplar, and willow. Less preferred but still acceptable are paper birch, cherry, elm, hickory, hornbeam, maple, and sassafras. Late-instar larvae will even devour things the earlier ones avoid, such as hemlock, pine, and spruce.

The good news is that there are a few plants that the caterpillars tend to avoid—ash, butternut, black walnut, catalpa, flowering dogwood, American holly, locust, sycamore, tulip tree, and such evergreens as arborvitae, balsam fir, mountain laurel, and rhododendron. At least these used to be avoided, but with every new outbreak there are reports of the caterpillars eating things they are not supposed to like. Evolution marches on.

When caterpillars have finished with one tree, they move on to the next. A grove of pure pine may be spared because there is not enough food in it to keep the young fed, but a single white pine surrounded by oaks is almost certain to be defoliated when older caterpillars have eaten all the oak leaves nearby.

To see a tree that was in full leaf in May suddenly bare in late June is a startling sight—or horrifying, depending on your point of view. What is just as startling is to see what happens three weeks later. Buds open and a second set of leaves appears. These leaves are often smaller and a lighter shade of green than the first ones, but the tree is in leaf and most definitely alive. Responding to the loss of its first set, the tree has merely dug down into its reserves of stored energy and manufactured a second set. Independence Day rumors that the trees are all dead have usually been forgotten by Labor Day.

Some of the trees do die—if not this year, then the next. Hemlocks that have lost all their needles usually die at once. Most other trees that die, however, are already in poor condition: Their roots were cut off when the driveway was built; they have absorbed too much road salt; they are diseased; they are growing in too much shade; they have been defoliated three years running. When a tree has no energy left and it is attacked by gypsy moths, it dies. But most trees do not. Even white pines have a 75 percent chance of surviving the loss of all their needles. Most other species—especially if they are growing on moist, fertile soil instead of dry rock—have an even better chance of survival.

Certain people, notably the manufacturers of pesticides, speak of the gypsy moths' "substantial alteration of the ecology," and they claim that "the balance of nature is radically upset." They are joined by campers whose campsites have been skeletonized, by drivers whose scenic vistas are not so scenic. Yet I can't see that gypsy moths have prevented the forest from returning to New England. The foresters I talk to don't regard the gypsy moth as apocalyptic. They tell me that the first time a forest is hit by gypsy moths, a sizable percentage of trees are killed—especially if there are successive years of defoliation—but subsequent outbreaks never kill as many. The weak trees have been weeded out. In many cases, the trees that die would die anyway before they reached maturity. Defoliation simply compresses the mortality into fewer years. Even if all the susceptible species were to be killed outright, species that the gypsy moth *didn't* eat would be favored. But so far, after one hundred years, there isn't much evidence that gypsy moths have affected forest composition. When asked about the importance of controlling gypsy moths, one forest economist put it simply, "Losses just aren't high enough to justify any effort."

Why, then, has more than $100 million been spent over the years on trying to stop the gypsy moth? The gypsy moth isn't really a pest of trees, it's a pest of people. People are disgusted when caterpillars cover the shingles of their house. They'd sooner have a rat crawl up their pants leg. People don't even like stepping on caterpillars as they stroll down the sidewalk. If the gypsy moth resided only in deep forest, no one would notice—but it flourishes in suburbia.

People in suburbia see trees differently than foresters do. They cherish every one. It is useless to speak of the probability that a certain tree will die when the tree is in someone's backyard.

"It shades the house."

"Where else would we hang the swing?"

"Great Aunt Myrtle's ashes are buried underneath."

You are talking about a personal asset, a friend, a monument, not about board feet of lumber. And so county agents are consulted, and arborists are hired to spray the trees. Among the insecticides they may use are carbaryl (Sevin), acephate (Orthene), or trichlorfon (Dylox). These sprays kill lots of different kinds of insects. Some people are concerned about this, especially about its effect on honeybees and on the food supply for birds. So next year they start earlier and hire someone to spray Bt (*Bacillus thuringiensis*), a bacterium that kills all kinds of butterfly and moth larvae but not much else. It has to be applied shortly after the eggs hatch, and perhaps a second time, and it's more expensive, but at least it spares the honeybees.

Others, caught between extreme environmentalism and concern for their white oak, resort to manual eradication. They try to scrape off all the egg masses into kerosene, or paint them over with creosote or diluted shellac. The larvae that hatch, they pick off and squash. A strip of burlap tied around the trunk traps the ones that are looking for a place to rest. A band of Tanglefoot, one of several commercially available sticky substances, keeps caterpillars from climbing the tree, but tree-lovers are careful to spread it on a strip of tar paper and tie the tar paper around the tree with cotton stuffed beneath, lest the sticky stuff cause the trunk to develop a canker. Keeping trees well watered and fertilized also helps them to survive.

By early July, when people are just beginning to get desperate, the eating stops. The caterpillars, after spinning the flimsiest of cocoons, pupate, transforming themselves into large brown teardrops, the female's larger than the male's. Even the most beleaguered homeowners begin to relax and recover. The caterpillars may be missing, but, of course, the gypsy moth's life cycles on. Ten to fourteen days later, the pupae split open and the moths emerge. The males, which emerge first and are slightly smaller, are brown; the females are white speckled with black. Neither merits being collected for its looks.

The female cannot even fly. Instead, she waits near the spot where she pupated and releases from her abdomen a pheromone—a sex attractant that has been identified as cis -7,8 -epoxy -2-methyloctadecane. To a male gypsy moth, this spells love. Hundreds of yards away, he detects a few molecules of the scent with his fernlike antennae and begins to fly upwind in a pattern that has earned him the French nickname *le Zigzag*.

Shortly after mating, the female lays from 75 to 1,000 eggs in a single mass and covers them over with the buff hairs from her abdomen. Two to four days after emerging from their pupae, and without ever having fed as adults, both males and females die. The embryo in each egg reaches full development in three weeks but, instead of hatching in August, remains quiescent until spring.

In nature, the egg masses stay put, but in suburbia, it's another story. People move during the summer. A family in New York State packs up to relocate in Wisconsin. Being thrifty, they take everything with them: the clothespole, the doghouse, the picnic table, even the leftover firewood. They don't see the furry tan patches stuck to their belongings.

Next spring, the eggs hatch and, a few years later, gypsy moths are well established where they never were before. If the town is lucky, some of the male moths will be captured in one of the 150,000 small, sticky traps, baited with synthetic sex attractant, set out by the Department of Agriculture all over the country to monitor the spread of the gypsy moth. This brings in the exterminators. Sometimes the exterminators are successful, sometimes they aren't. In 1973, a house trailer carried eggs from Connecticut to Michigan, and in spite of intense efforts to get rid of them, the moths seem to be there to stay.

This close association between humans and gypsy moths dates back to the moth's introduction to this country. Leopold Trouvelot, astronomer, naturalist, and entrepreneur, was apparently trying to breed a disease-resistant silkworm for the silk industry of his native France by crossing the gypsy moth with the silk moth. Since the gypsy moth is native to Europe (and North Africa and Asia), he should have conducted his experiments there, but in 1868 he happened to be living outside Boston, at 27 Myrtle Street, in the suburb of Medford. In the two-story clapboard house with a picket fence in front and a grape arbor out back, he began to rear gypsy moths. No one knows how it happened, but within a year some of his charges had escaped.

However much we may regret his actions today, we should note that his motives were as well intentioned as— and considerably more sensible than—those of Eugene Scheifflin, a wealthy New York City drug manufacturer who introduced forty pairs of starlings into Central Park in 1890 because he wished to establish in this country every species of bird mentioned by Shakespeare. It is to Trouvelot's credit that he recognized the omnivorous appetites of his escapees and notified the authorities. Scheifflin, on the other hand, released forty more starlings a year later, and now the pests infest the entire United States.

With an abundance of food, the escaped gypsy moths prospered, and, by 1880, their descendants occupied 400 square miles. Around the Trouvelot house they were especially troublesome, but Trouvelot had returned to Paris and the caterpillars were assumed to be some native species. It was not until 1889 that the first major outbreak occurred. There have been many population explosions since then, but none will be remembered like the summer of '89, when the caterpillars rampaged through Medford.

Mrs. F. T. Spinney, the wife of Medford's postmaster, remembered what happened: "I lived on Cross Street in 1889. In June of that year, I was out of town for three days. When I went away, the trees in our yard were in splendid condition, and there was not a sign of insect devastation upon them. When I returned, there was scarcely a leaf upon the trees. The gypsy moth caterpillars were over everything."

"The caterpillars were so thick on the trees," added J.

P. Dill, "that they were stuck together like cold macaroni."

Mrs. Thomas F. Mayo, living at 25 Myrtle Street, joined the women on the street and together they made a regular business of killing caterpillars. "The caterpillars used to cover the basement and clapboards of the house as high as the windowsill. They lay in a solid black mass. I would scrape them off into an old dishpan holding about 10 quarts. When it was two-thirds full, I poured kerosene over the mass of worms and set them on fire. I used to do this a number of times a day. It was sickening work."

The official response was immediate, and on March 14, 1890, the Massachusetts legislature appropriated $25,000 to control the gypsy moth. Men were sent aloft to scrape egg masses off even the highest branches of the largest elms. Stone walls were burned, trees were burlapped, Paris green (a compound of copper and arsenic) was sprayed from horse-drawn wagons.

The results are history. A "barrier zone" 30 miles wide was established between Long Island Sound and the Canadian border in 1923, and it failed completely. Even C-47 transport planes spraying 150 gallons of DDT a minute in 600-foot-wide swaths couldn't kill all the caterpillars. Like a scoop of ice cream melting on a summer sidewalk, the gypsy moths have continued to spread. On the map of gypsy moth distribution, the shaded portion now extends west nearly to Ohio and south to Maryland.

In 1980, five million acres were defoliated by gypsy moths. Of course, these acres were not all contiguous. Damage tends to occur in a mosaic, a moth-eaten patchwork quilt. Adjacent to a patch of forest that has been heavily grazed, there may be another virtually untouched. How abundant the caterpillars are depends partly on the recent local history of the moth. Where moths have been particularly abundant, epidemics of disease are likely to cause their numbers to decline. In other areas, where the moths used to be scarce, their numbers suddenly increase at irregular intervals for currently inexplicable reasons—a phenomenon that bedevils scientists trying to understand the ecology of gypsy moths.

The Department of Agriculture is in charge of preventing the gypsy moth's spread, of identifying and eradicating those pockets of gypsy moths that appear regularly way out beyond the major front. But these efforts are only a holding action. There is no reason to believe that the gypsy moth will not someday occur everywhere that there is deciduous forest, from Florida to California.

Central to the success of the gypsy moths in this country is the fact that they have escaped from their natural enemies. Throughout the species' natural range from Portugal to Japan, there are places where the population periodically explodes, but such outbreaks tend to be infrequent and short-lived. The gypsy moths are always at the mercy of parasites, predators, and disease, and for years at a stretch are too scarce to cause any problems.

From the first, the importation of natural enemies was part of gypsy moth control. "Civilized man should have the advantage of the savage in being able to use one force of nature against another," wrote Edward R. Farrar, the tree warden of Lincoln, Massachusetts, in 1906; and since then, more than forty-five natural enemies of the gypsy moth have been introduced in the United States. Most have died out, in some cases because of the lack of an intermediate host, but at least ten parasites and one predator, a greenish black ground beetle, are now established here.

In a given season, a female of *Oencyrtus kuvanae*, a tiny wasp from Japan, can destroy two hundred gypsy moth eggs, while a female *Apanteles melanoscelus*, a wasp from Europe, can kill 1,000 caterpillars. The tachinid fly, *Blepharipa pratensis*, is even more destructive, laying 5,000 or more eggs on the foliage of infested trees. Gypsy-moth caterpillars accidentally swallow these tiny time bombs when they are feeding. The eggs hatch and the maggots consume the caterpillars from within.

All but one of these parasites were successfully introduced before 1930. Misplaced optimism that DDT was going to eradicate gypsy moths once and for all led to a reduced interest in biological control. But the questionable effectiveness of aerial spraying and its unquestionably high cost have prompted a renewed interest in the gypsy moth's natural enemies. Laboratories in Paris and Sapporo, Japan, are devoted to searching for new parasites. Hundreds are thought to exist, and all of China remains to be explored.

The best-known disease that afflicts the gypsy moth is wilt disease, so-named because of the inverted V in which the dying caterpillar hangs. The disease was accidentally introduced to this country and epidemics of it have caused dense populations to crash. Laboratory-reared caterpillars are being infected with the nuclear polyhedrosis virus that causes the disease, and their bodies are then freeze-dried and ground up to produce a spray called Gypchek that the Forest Service hopes will cause premature collapse of exploding populations.

Finally, there are predators. A host of native animals have developed tastes for gypsy moths. Chickadees, blue jays, and robins will all feed on sparse populations, while flocking species such as crows, grackles, and red-winged blackbirds are attracted to areas where there are dense ones. Even Eugene Scheifflin's starlings, reviled for their bullying of smaller birds and their clogging of jet engines, deserve some credit for eating large numbers of caterpillars, pupae, and adult moths.

People like having birds in their backyards, but they are less fond of mice. Yet the white-footed mouse, the most common small mammal in the Northeast, eats enormous numbers of gypsy-moth caterpillars, carefully rolling back the skin like a sock to avoid the sharp hairs.

Unfortunately, mice like to live where there are brush piles, dense leaf litter, and stone walls. So do many other animals that feed on gypsy moths: chipmunks, squirrels, shrews, moles, skunks, raccoons, and opossums. Yet in most backyards, what might become predator habitat is sawed up and burned or raked up and dumped into plastic trash bags. Gypsy moths flourish in a well-manicured backyard. Their predators do not.

It is now clear that the gypsy moth will cross any artificial barrier we create, and that it will survive every attempt at extermination. I don't like gypsy moths, I never have. But since we have failed to repel the beast, I propose that we make every effort to convert it from a foreign visitor to a naturalized citizen. If its presence here becomes normal, its numbers may, too. Let us burden the gypsy moth with all the life-shortening benefits of citizenship, with the insect equivalents of such things as military service and taxation. Constant pressure from predators, parasites, and disease offers the best chance to control the number of gypsy moths. This will mean continuing to scour Europe and Asia for pests of the gypsy moth. It will mean refraining from poisoning the gypsy-moth pests we already have with the indiscriminate use of insecticides. It may also mean leaving the grass long, the leaves unraked, and the skunk nesting under the back steps.

This is not to suggest a passive policy of letting nature take its course. We never have and probably never will. Right now, dirty tricks are popular—using synthetic sex attractants to confuse male gypsy moths or releasing laboratory-reared sterile males to fool the females. This sort of activity is fine so long as it doesn't hinder the efforts of the other organisms, many of whom are better equipped to kill gypsy moths than we will ever be. We should concentrate on encouraging the gypsy moth's natural enemies, seeing to it that gypsy moths are subject to every predator, parasite, and disease there is. The wild swinging of the population pendulum will diminish once the gypsy moth is truly established in this country.

As the leaves disappear, and as caterpillar droppings rain down, many people may think that the gypsy moth is already too well established. It isn't. Not yet. But soon, when wilted caterpillars begin to appear, pupae fail to hatch, and egg masses have only 200 instead of 1,000 eggs in them, it will be a sign that the population is about to crash. Biological controls will bring the gypsy moths within bounds, and only biological controls can keep them there. What's needed at a time like this is to extend our love of animals to every snake, toad, or ant that feeds on gypsy moths. Someday there may come a time when gypsy-moth caterpillars are so uncommon that children will collect them, bringing them home in glass jars to keep as pets.

9

BARE HARVARD

Inasmuch as the debate took place where it did, the entire affair was cordial, rational, civilized—in short, Harvard. Gathered at the venerable statue of John Harvard one sunny day in May 1982, scores of students and faculty members were protesting plans to remove the ivy from the facades of several buildings. Shouting, "Hell, no! Let the Ivy Grow!" and waving signs that read, "What Do You Think Ivy League Means, Anyway?" the Friday afternoon crowd heard speeches, testimonials, and an oration in Latin on the virtues of ivy. Someone climbed onto John Harvard's lap and placed an ivy wreath on his head. Although some of the newly sown grass seed was trampled, there was none of the anger that has characterized demonstrations at college campuses in the past: no bricks were thrown, no fists raised, no insults uttered. One woman said this was the first rally at which she did not feel she had to be outraged. Even the dean of the college, on whose doorstep the event was staged, praised his opponents, saying he had never heard rhetoric that was so rational or so well researched.

Both sides agreed that the ivy will have to be pulled down so that contractors can work on renovating the undergraduate residences. At issue was whether the ivy would be allowed to ascend again after the work was completed, or whether it would be poisoned at the roots, leaving the walls forever bare. The students, surprisingly, found themselves on the side of tradition, wanting walls shingled with the shiny, dark green, three-lobed leaves. The administration was quick to point out that the tradition of ivy-covered walls is comparatively young. No college has had ivy for more than 120 years, for the vine *Parthenocissus tricuspidata* was not introduced into the United States until 1862.

The species is native to Japan and central China, and was originally sold by nurseries as Japanese ivy. Its immediate success in its adopted homeland, where some called it the horticultural find of the century, caused it to be rechristened Boston ivy. Like many other eastern Asian plants, *Parthenocissus tricuspidata* has a close relation in eastern North America. *Parthenocissus quinquefolia*, the Virginia creeper, or woodbine, grows wild in woods and along roadsides from Maine to Florida. Technically speaking, neither vine is a true ivy, since both belong to the grape family. This matters only to botanists, except that the intimate association between Boston ivy and higher education has given fresh meaning to the axiom *in vino veritas*.

Had the plant been introduced two centuries earlier, there would probably have been little interest in it. The Puritans, fearful of the wilderness on all sides, preferred bare earth to foundation plantings. By the late nineteenth century, the greenery had been pushed back far enough that members of a new profession, landscape architects, had set about winning back the beauty of nature by planting thickets of shrubs and vines close about buildings. For this, the new ivy was ideal.

Unlike the evergreen English ivy (which is a true ivy), Boston ivy is deciduous, shedding its leaves each winter. It is also much hardier than English ivy, surviving temperatures as low as minus 20 degrees Fahrenheit. Hence it can be grown everywhere in the United States except in the Great Plains and the extreme south, where heat and drought limit its growth. The plant is tolerant of urban pollution and grows rapidly—from 6 to 10 feet a year—with an ultimate reach of 60 feet. The tiny green flowers are inconspicuous, and followed by blue black fruit, but they are compensated for by glorious autumn foliage. "In sheer splendor there is no climbing plant that equals the Japanese ivy when it assumes its October garb," wrote Byron Halsted in a New Jersey Agricultural Experiment Stations Bulletin in 1900. "At its best it seems as if the Artist had dipped the giant brush in a harmonious mixture of crimson and gold and touched the walls in an earnest of Infinite purpose and perfection."

Other vines—bittersweet, clematis, wisteria—require some sort of trellis on which to climb. Boston ivy, however, can scale the smoothest wall without such assistance, using adhesive discs on the tips of its tendrils. As each new leaf develops, so does an adjacent tendril (except at every third node, where there is no tendril), which is negatively phototropic, growing away from the light. At the tips of the branches of the pale green tendrils are reddish swellings. Upon contacting a surface, each of these swellings expands radially, and its cuticle, or covering, bursts, releasing a gummy mucus rich in dextrin. In forty-eight to seventy-two hours this glue has hardened, cementing each of the five to ten discs of the tendril to the surface. The tendril then contracts into a spiral, pulling the vine in closer to the adhesive discs. Like a many-footed tree frog, Boston ivy can creep up vertical faces smooth enough to stymie the most expert rock climber.

Each tendril lives only one year, but even in death its grip is tenacious. Referring to the Virginia creeper, Charles Darwin wrote in 1867, "There are tendrils now adhering to my house which are still strong and have been exposed to the weather in a dead state for fourteen or fifteen years." A single disc, he found, supported a weight of 2 pounds. Years after the vines have been torn off walls, the discs remain—wizened, brown, sticky fingers that loose their grip only when soaked in ether.

By the time of the U.S. centennial celebration, in 1876, ivy was prevalent in Boston. But it was not planted at Harvard until about a decade later. Although there are no exact records, the evidence points to Charles Eliot, a young landscape architect and son of Harvard's president, who in 1887 was paid $500 by the treasurer of Harvard University for shrub plantations in the college Yard. Some note of the introduction of Boston ivy may be buried in Harvard's archives: it appears for the first time in photographs taken at Harvard in the late 1880s. By the turn of the century, President Eliot's small act of nepotism had spread to cover nearly all the walls of the college.

Harvard was probably not the first college to wear ivy, and certainly was not the last to assume the verdant mantle. On many campuses Boston ivy served both to camouflage unsightly buildings and to unify architecture of different styles. By the 1930s, Boston ivy was so much an academic institution that Caswell Adams, a sports writer at the New York *Herald Tribune*, coined the term Ivy League. (The intercollegiate athletic conference made up of Harvard, Yale, Pennsylvania, Princeton, Columbia, Brown, Dartmouth, and Cornell was formally inaugurated in 1956.)

While the Ivy League has flourished, becoming a symbol of academic and social prestige, some people have come to wish that the ivy itself had not done so well. Ivy does not stop growing simply because it has covered all the available masonry: it proceeds to cover windows and doors. Keeping it in its place takes annual pruning, an expense that can be hard on beleaguered budgets. Old vines as thick as a forearm are a temptation to young Tarzans, and sections of the vine periodically die back—at least once because a thief chose to cut a vine trunk rather than the bicycle chain secured to it. Finally, brickwork must be repointed every forty or fifty years, and for this to be done the vines must come down.

Some of those responsible for building maintenance, the ones who put the ladders up and take them down, are not as fond of the ivy as the faculty and the students are. Some want to see it banished for good, and the annual pruning along with it. Adding weight to this view is the contention of engineers that ivy is bad for walls. They say that it pulls off paint and rots woodwork.

It can even damage masonry. Particularly dense growths of it tend to trap moisture against the walls, and the decay of the adhesive discs and other organic matter yields humic acid capable of dissolving carbonate rock and lime mortar. Unrestrained, ivy will shift downspouts and burrow under flashing. Allowed to clamber onto the roof, it can raise up slate shingles and pull away cornices. Wherever a young shoot can penetrate a crack or a crevice, there is a chance that it will dislodge something.

Ivy is not, however, very high on the list of threats to higher education. Bare walls may last longer, but how much longer is something no one hazards to guess. It may be months, it may be years. At Dartmouth, the head of Buildings and Grounds has resolved to study his brickwork more carefully in the future; so far he has not seen any sign that Boston ivy is detrimental. Furthermore, there are obvious virtues to having ivy on walls, virtues acknowledged even by those who have to contend with it. First, and foremost, is the matter of aesthetics. Some naked walls are just plain ugly. The last century had no monopoly on unsightly architecture, and Boston ivy continues to be planted on many college campuses to ameliorate expanses of bare masonry.

Moreover, the ivy supports a diversity of wildlife. Much of the year it becomes a two-dimensional bird sanctuary, a place to roost, to nest, to feed on the ripe fruits. Some students sitting by open windows are glad for the distraction of even an eight-spotted forester moth, whose larvae feed on the leaves of *Parthenocissus*. These black, day-flying moths with their white and yellow polka-dotted wings have fuzzy orange legs, as though they were still wearing their warm-up socks. Finally, defenders of ivy who want to confront the engineers head on point out that the water evaporating from the leaves of the ivy cools the building during the summer, as does the insulating airspace between the leaves and the masonry.

Although debate over ivy provides a welcome respite from more serious issues, college administrators might as well agree to allow the ivy to grow on masonry walls subject to the following conditions: it should not be allowed to reach the eaves and should be kept well away from paint, wood, and other delicate surfaces. Sections of the ivy should be periodically removed altogether, to allow for repointing or other repairs to the underlying wall and to prevent the buildup of excessive organic matter. In either event, the ivy should be allowed to regenerate. This would please everyone. The design-conscious will acknowledge that no landscape is static, and the engineering-minded will admit that a thin coat of ivy hangs lightly and harmlessly on any wall.

College administrations that persist in trying to eliminate the ivy completely will find this to be as impractical as allowing it to grow rampant. Harvard is not the first college to try going ivy-less. Michigan State tore down the ivy from one building, exposing itself to such criticism that plans for further defoliation were shelved. At Harvard, the defenders of ivy will, if necessary, take their cause to the supreme court, in this case the alumni. Returning each year to celebrate commencement, the alumni expect to find the ivy just as it was. None of them, not even the oldest living graduate, can remember bare Harvard. Most have a deep affection for Boston ivy, one that may have required four years to take root but that has done well ever since. What is college after all, if not an ivy tower?

IO

MULBERRY VISIONS

God in the whizzing of a pleasant wind
Shall march upon the tops of mulberry trees.
GEORGE PEELE
(1558–1597)

Pedaling to nowhere special, a flock of children stops under a mulberry tree whose limbs arch over the sidewalk. Some stand on their bicycles to reach the fruits that have turned from white, to pink, to purply black, while the less agile ones pick up those that the wind has blown onto the edge of the front lawn. The bicycle perchers eat their berries one at a time; those gleaning in the grass can save up whole handfuls and mouth them at once. Either way, the small, sweet, blackberrylike fruits bruise so easily that they leave a trail of purple stain from faces to fingertips. Within minutes, all of the mulberry eaters look as though they have been mimeographed.

Some of them will be scolded for coming home purple. For the moment, however, they are on safe ground. The

86

owners of the mulberry trees aren't going to chase them away. During mulberry season, which lasts for nearly two months, from July to September, the husband objects only to the birds that come to feed in the tree and anoint his lawn furniture. His wife spends every morning sweeping up the fallen fruits before they stain the patio. They are a typical couple. They don't like mulberries.

One wonders whether they realize that they have a relic growing on their front lawn. And if they knew this, would it restore some of their enthusiasm for the fruit, an enthusiasm they must have had when they were children?

For at least forty-five hundred years the leaves of mulberry trees have been fed to caterpillars of *Bombyx mori*, the silk moth. After five or six weeks of feeding on mulberry leaves, the silkworms spin cocoons about the size of pullet eggs, each consisting of a single filament of silk ½ mile long. If the adult silk moth, a creamy-white insect with a 2-inch wingspan, were allowed to emerge, it would break the filament, so it must be killed prematurely with steam or hot air. Then, after the end of the filament on each cocoon is located, several are unwound at once, the individual filaments being combined and reeled up as a single, thicker thread. This in turn is doubled and twisted to form a still thicker strand, which eventually can be used to manufacture anything from hair ribbons to silk stockings.

Both the silkworm and the species of mulberry that it prefers to feed on are native to China, where silk production, or sericulture, remained a closely guarded secret until about A.D. 550. Then, encouraged by the Emperor Justinian, two former missionaries smuggled silkworm eggs and mulberry seeds to Constantinople, hidden inside hollow canes. From Byzantium, the Moors carried silk culture to North Africa in the eighth century, and later on to Spain. By the thirteenth century, Italians were spinning their own silk, and in successive centuries the industry spread to France and England.

Early colonists of America thought the land had all the attributes of China. In 1621 the London Company sent silkworm eggs to Virginia along with a shipment of European wine grapes intended for a vineyard along the James River. The company imposed a fine of 10 pounds of tobacco on every planter who did not maintain at least ten mulberry trees for every 100 acres of land, and the governor offered a reward of 50 pounds of tobacco for each pound of silk produced. In 1660, the coronation robes of Charles II were made of Virginia silk.

When new settlements were founded to the south, in Georgia and the Carolinas, mulberries and silkworms were introduced with equal enthusiasm. The most successful were a group of German Protestants, the Salzburgers, who lived 25 miles above Savannah. In 1751, they sent to England 1,000 pounds of raw cocoons and 74 pounds and 2 ounces of raw silk, a shipment worth £100. Today such a sum is unimpressive, but at the time £20 was enough to buy a modest frame house.

The successes, however, were short-lived, for cotton proved to be a more lucrative crop, and those southerners who persisted in growing silk were mostly wiped out by the upheavals of the American Revolution.

Although northern silk production survived the Revolution, it went into a decline shortly thereafter. Whereas large mulberry groves once flourished in Princeton, New

Jersey, and Boston and New Haven had competed in raising cocoons and spinning and dyeing the raw silk, silk hus-
bandry had almost ceased by 1800. Then, for some unex-
plained reason, there was fresh enthusiasm for silk culture.
State legislatures got into the act. In 1831, the Common-
wealth of Massachusetts paid Jonathan Cobb of Dedham
$600 to write a "concise Manual, to contain the best infor-
mation respecting the growth of the Mulberry tree, with
suitable directions for the culture of silk."

This renewed interest in silk was both dependent on
and responsible for the widespread planting of a new type
of mulberry tree. The new mulberry was called *Morus
multicaulis*. The nation's previous failure to rival Europe
and the Orient in the manufacture of silk was blamed on
feeding silkworms the wrong type of leaves. Although silkworms will feed on most species of mulberries, they have
their preferences. Neither the leaves of the red mulberry
(*Morus rubra*), which is native to the forests of the eastern
United States, nor the leaves of the black mulberry (*Morus
nigra*), grown for its fruit in Europe, are quite as suitable
for silk as are the leaves of the white mulberry (*Morus
alba*) from China. (Unfortunately, the color of the fruit is
not a sure way to identify the species, because different
white mulberry trees have ripe fruit that is white, red, or
black.) White mulberry trees were what most Americans
and Europeans had been raising all along. The new mulberry was one that Georges Samuel Perrottet had introduced to France from the Philippines in 1824. It was called
Morus multicaulis ("many-stemmed"), from its habit of
sending up numerous shoots from ground level. When this
tree reached Long Island, in 1829, it was accompanied by

the belief that this was the true source of Chinese silk. Silk, it was said, would soon be produced as cheaply as cotton.

Gripped by what came to be known as "the Multi-caulis Craze," nurserymen gave up offering anything else. One man sailed to the West Indies to raise a few hundred thousand plants over the winter, to take advantage of the demand. The new mulberry was planted even in the thinly settled parts of the West and as far north as Maine.

Then disaster struck. The market for young trees became overstocked. A hard winter proved that *Morus multicaulis* (called *Morus alba* var. *multicaulis* today) was less hardy than people thought, and a disease appeared. Nurseries went bankrupt. Mulberry trees that had once commanded more than a dollar apiece were sold for pea brush at a dollar a hundred. Millions of others were simply abandoned. Some silk continued to be produced, but the labor ultimately proved to be too costly for this country to compete with Europe and Asia. Today we have a booming silk industry, but it is a synthetic one, requiring neither silkworms nor mulberries.

Once they were no longer needed for silk, the silkworms, totally dependent on human attention for their survival, virtually vanished. The mulberry trees, however, have continued to flourish unattended, thanks in part to the birds whose droppings have assured generation after generation of seedlings. Today the second most common weed tree in New York City is the white mulberry. (Curiously, the number-one weed tree is also the legacy of silken dreams: ailanthus, or tree of heaven, was introduced to this country along with the ailanthus moth [*Samia walkeri*], because the latter spins a coarse grade of silk.)

While acknowledging its messy fruit and its weediness,

there are those who nevertheless think the white mulberry is the perfect street tree for city landscaping—fast growing, virtually pest-free, and tolerant of drought, pollution, adverse soil conditions, and pH. Because some mulberries are all male or all female, several fruitless selections of white mulberry are now available, among them 'Kingan' and 'Striblingii'.

The Russian mulberry, *Morus alba* 'Tatarica', was introduced into the western United States by Russian Mennonites in 1875. It proved to be not only the hardiest mulberry of all but a good windbreak as well. In 1883 an unusual seedling of the Russian mulberry appeared in the nursery row of John C. Teas of Carthage, Missouri. Cuttings from this plant, when grafted onto a head-high Russian mulberry stock, resulted in the famous 'Teas' Weeping' mulberry, whose cascading branches graced many a Victorian home's front lawn.

Any catalog of uses for mulberry trees would have to include fenceposts and firewood and cabinetwork. It is even possible to make a cloth from the fibers contained in young shoots, in the manner of processing flax into linen. But at the top of any such list should be eating the fruit.

Even when mulberry trees were being grown primarily for silk, there were people who considered them useful as fruit trees. Of course the English have a tradition of eating mulberries—mulberry-and-apple jam, mulberry syrup, mulberry vinegar, cold mulberry pie. But when they speak of mulberries, they are speaking of the fruit of *Morus nigra*, the black mulberry. Black mulberries have been grown in this country under various names, such as 'Persian', 'Black Persian', and the 'Black Mulberry of Spain', but these trees are reliably hardy only in the South and on the Pacific Coast. From the English point of view, *Morus alba* fruits are small, insipid, and unfit for eating. Although many of them are, the species is enormously variable, not only in the shape of the leaves but in the size, color, and quality of the fruit. During the nineteenth century, various selections of *Morus alba* yielded mulberries whose fruits rivaled the best of any black mulberry. Among these was even a survivor of the Multicaulis Craze. Of the 'Downing' mulberry, discovered in 1846, Henry Ward Beecher wrote, "I regard it to be an indispensable addition to every fruit-garden; and I speak what I think when I say that I had rather have one tree of Downing's Everbearing Mulberries than a bed of strawberries." Unfortunately, this mulberry shared its ancestors' sensitivity to cold and could only be grown in the South.

This mulberry may, in fact, no longer exist. Even fifty years ago nurseries offering it were actually selling 'New American' mulberry trees. A seedling white mulberry that was first offered for sale about 1854, 'New American' is considered the best northern mulberry tree grown for its fruit. It is probably a 'New American' under which the children's bicycles are parked, the fruits being a glossy black and nearly 2 inches long.

Mulberry cultivars have become badly confused, in part because there has not been much demand. The New York State Fruit Testing Association sells a mulberry tree that they call 'Wellington' after Richard Wellington, in whose yard adjacent to the fruit-testing station the parent tree is growing. But they admit that it may well be the 'New American'. After so many years of neglect one can only wonder what has happened to other white mulberry trees selected for their fruit: 'Lampasas', 'Ramsey White', 'Trowbridge', 'Thornburn', and 'Victoria'.

Although in the North the best mulberries are all cultivars of the white mulberry, in the South they are mostly cultivars of the native red mulberry. 'Hicks' is perhaps the best known. 'Johnson' was said to be the largest of any mulberry, but along with 'Stubbs', 'Townsend', and 'Travis' it may have been lost.

The disappearance of named cultivars from nursery catalogs, and indeed from nurseries themselves, is a shame. "The mulberry is easily the king of tree crops," claimed J. Russell Smith, professor of economic geography at Columbia University. A fervent champion of growing trees to reduce soil erosion, he lobbied hard to encourage more people to plant mulberries. In his *Tree Crops: A Permanent Agriculture* (1950), he ticks off their virtues: easy to propagate, grow rapidly, bear early and regularly as far north as New England, have a long fruiting season. He notes further that the tree is unusual both in that it bears fruit in the shady parts of the tree as well as the sunny, and in that it can recover from frost to the extent of making a partial crop the same year by putting forth a second set of buds to replace the first ones.

The fruits can also be fed to pigs and chickens. On a long journey through the Cotton Belt in 1913, Smith collected numerous testimonials to the virtue of the mulberry. Most farmers were in agreement that a mulberry tree could feed a hog for at least two months. As one Carolinian said, "I wouldn't take a pretty fer my mulberry orchard. It's funny to me to see how soon a hawg kin learn that wind blows down the mulberries. Soon as the wind starts up, Mr. Hawg strikes a trot out of the woods fer the mulberry grove. Turn yer pigs into mulberries, and they shed off and slick up nice. It puts 'em in fine shape—conditions 'em like turnin' 'em in on wheat. They eats mulberries and goes down to the branch and cools off, and come backs and eats more—don't need any grain in mulberry time."

Lest it seem improbable that so much ham and bacon could result from eating such small fruit, consider the Afghan villagers who, as recently as a hundred years ago, subsisted on a mixture of dried seedless white mulberries and ground almonds for eight months of the year. Dried, the mulberries are as nutritious as their family relation the fig.

I propose to experiment with mulberries as fruit. I haven't given up trying to grow peaches, pears, and apples, but I have decided that the ones in the store are a bargain. Mulberries aren't sold in stores and aren't likely to be unless they become much tougher and less perishable. Their obscurity is undeserved, for they are unaffected by late frosts, fire blight, or coddling moths. Even with complete neglect they continue to shower the sidewalks with perfect fruit summer after summer. If the only flaw in this utopian fruit is the lackluster taste, I'll either learn to like it as it is or find a tree with better flavor. It's true that many mulberries aren't worth a second taste, but with millions of wild seedlings to choose from, there ought to be a few dozen that deserve perpetuating.

Nurseries were once clearinghouses for the better mulberry cultivars, but if we all tried to order mulberry trees today, there wouldn't be enough. Instead, we would get notices saying, "We are temporarily out of stock." You can't blame the nurseries. Mulberry trees haven't been very popular lately, and mulberry trees aren't something that can be stored away like nose bags and washboards until the demand returns. If they have parent trees handy, the nurseries are quite capable of producing thousands of mulberry trees, given a couple of years' notice. But it will be quite understandable if, this time, they don't rush.

Those of us who can't wait may end up helping ourselves. Mulberry seeds will germinate readily, provided they have first been mixed with damp sand and placed in a tightly tied polyethylene bag in a refrigerator at 40 degrees Fahrenheit for three months. However, seedlings are notoriously variable, and it will be safer to start with a plant we like, rooting softwood or hardwood cuttings or grafting onto seedling rootstocks. Or we can simply dig up and move the tree. Mulberries are unlikely ever to be in such demand that the trees can't be had for the asking.

As for the risk of moving an older mulberry, J. Russell Smith quotes another Carolinian: "Yeh can't kill the things. . . . I moved a tree last yeah. Jest put a man to cuttin' roots off—and he cut 'em scandalous—and I hooked two mules to it and hauled it ovah heah. I didn't 'spect it would live, but it did." Apparently, the danger in moving big mulberry trees is to the lower back, not to the tree.

I intend to plant a mulberry tree. In a few years the birds and the bicycles will be in our backyard. When the sun sets and the clamor has ceased, I will serve mulberry Bavarian cream on the deck with homemade mulberry wine. There will always be some people who can't be persuaded to eat mulberries. I'll have to entertain them by pointing out that the mulberry tree is an ingredient of both silk purses and sows' ears.

II

<hr>

BEE BITES

At dinner last evening, the woman across from me was describing how swollen her arm had been after three bee bites. "Mosquitoes bite," I corrected her, "honeybees sting." I was tempted to add something about asses and elbows, but manners prevailed. My distinction was dismissed with a toss of bracelets, and she went on to explain that her doctor had warned her that she was allergic to bees.

Rebuffed, I returned to dissecting my pork chop. Eleven-year-olds can describe precisely the armament on an F-14 Tomcat. ("The world's deadliest combat aircraft. A 20-mm rotary cannon with 675 rounds. External load of 14,500 pounds of bombs and combinations of Phoenix, Sparrow, and Sidewinder air-to-air missiles.") Yet most adults have difficulty distinguishing the front end of an insect from its rear. Why is information about human weaponry collected with the same enthusiasm as baseball cards when information about insect weaponry is so overlooked? As a deterrent, at least as a deterrent to going outdoors, insects are far more effective than F-14s.

People remain unenlightened about insects for two reasons. Although most of them have run into bees, wasps, or ants, they are usually too excited by the encounter to take notes. When a yellow jacket is sucked in the car's window vent, the driver is apt to be too busy running off the road to notice whether he is being bitten or stung. These distinctions are better made either before or after the encounter, but then the curious run into a lack of information, or at least a lack of accessible information. Robert Snodgrass has written a fine book called *The Anatomy of the Honey Bee*, but it is 334 pages long and not likely to be a best seller or even an editor's choice.

The woman across from me, newly convalescent from an encounter with *Apis mellifera*, was clearly in need of more information. It would amuse her and fascinate her to learn more about honeybee stings. She would welcome the instruction and find the knowledge useful. I waited until dessert was served, and then I began.

"You know," I said, pointing my spoon at her, "only females sting. It's because the sting of a bee or wasp or an ant is a modified ovipositor. The ovipositor, which in most insects is used to pierce and deposit eggs inside something, has evolved into a device for injecting venom. Since only females lay eggs, only females sting. The bad news is that in colonies of bees, wasps, and ants, almost all the members are females."

Afraid that I was beginning to sound like a misogynist, I smiled warmly and hurried on.

"The sting of a honeybee is a shaft with a bulbous base. The shaft is made of three separate pieces: a stylet and two lancets. The three pieces are neatly fitted together to form a central tube called a poison canal. Venom is manufactured by two glands that empty into a poison sac, which in turn empties into the bulb at the base of the sting."

I looked around for a napkin on which to draw a diagram. Finding only linen, I had to forgo the visual aids.

"When a honeybee stings you, she bends her abdomen sharply downward and extrudes the sting that is ordinarily concealed in a sting chamber. With a quick jab, she sticks the tip of the sting into you. The two lancets have barbed tips and, furthermore, are capable of being moved independently. Muscles attached to the sting contract in rapid alternation advancing the lancets, the barbs on one securing it while the other is pushed in deeper. Meanwhile, the same muscles that are embedding the sting are also pumping venom down the poison canal where it escapes through a cleft near the tip of the sting shaft."

The woman across from me was looking pained. Her banana pudding lay untouched.

"What did you do when you were stung?" I inquired.

"I screamed," she replied, "and swatted at it. When I opened my eyes it was gone."

Beside me a freckle-faced child with gaps in her teeth chimed in: "The sting wasn't. Bees lose their stings and then they die." She looked at me for confirmation.

"That's right." I beamed at her, delighted to have a partner in my educational endeavor. "Although wasps can sting you over and over, a honeybee can only sting you once. Your soft skin grips the barbs on the lancets too tightly for the bee to withdraw them. If the bee were to sting another insect, she wouldn't lose her sting, but if she stings a soft-skinned animal like you, the entire sting apparatus rips right out of her. It isn't very strongly attached in the first place, and as she flies off, she leaves her sting behind, often with a few attached innards."

At the mention of innards, other people seemed to become interested. At least they put down their spoons.

"The most remarkable thing about the honeybee sting is that it's like an automatic hypodermic syringe. Even after the bee has flown away, the muscles attached to the sting keep working it in deeper and deeper and keep pumping in venom. If you remove the sting from yourself in a few seconds, you'll cut way down on the amount of venom that's injected. It's no good to grab the sting between your fingers, because you'll just squeeze the rest of the venom into you. It would be like grabbing the top of an eyedropper. Instead, take your fingernail and scrape the sting out. If your fingernails are too short, use a penknife blade or a nail file. You'll find that the sting comes out easily.

"From the bee's point of view, having a sting that tears out, even if it is ultimately fatal, is a neat way to guarantee that more venom gets into the victim. If she had to hang around, she might be brushed off prematurely. In general, of course, bees don't sting people. You have to be disturbing the hive to get attacked, or else step on or bump into an individual bee somewhere. Even if you throw rocks at a beehive, less than half of one percent of the bees in the hive are likely to sting. Alarmed bees look for movement and color, and at close range, odor. Dark clothing, hair, and leather elicit stinging. Away from the hive, brightly colored clothing and sweet perfumes may attract a bee, and chemicals in a person's breath may cause her to sting.

"I don't suppose you smelled your arm after the bee stung you?" I asked the woman across the table. From her expression, I gathered she hadn't.

"When the sting tears out of the bee, an alarm pheromone is released, a chemical that signals other bees to come and attack. If there are other bees in the vicinity, one sting is likely to lead to others. Guess what the chemical is?" I brandished the remains of my banana pudding. "It's isoamyl acetate. You can smell it anytime; just go to the garden and mash a bee and sniff its abdomen. Straight banana oil."

I paused to finish the pudding in my cup and noticed that the others had resumed eating. But I could see they were doing so cautiously.

"Now the venom that's being pumped into you is remarkable stuff," I continued. "There's not much of it, less than 0.3 milligrams, and most of that is water, but the rest is a mix of at least 10 ingredients. There are some low-molecular-weight agents like histamine, dopamine, and noradrenaline. There are also some high-molecular-weight toxins like the hemolyzing melittin, a neurotoxic apamin, mast-cell-degranulating peptide, and minimine, and there are some enzymes like phospholipase A and B, and hyaluronidase. The various ways in which these compounds affect a person's body are still being worked out, but there's hope that some of them will prove to be medically useful.

"The idea that bee venom might be beneficial goes back at least to the ancient Greeks. Since then a lot of people have used bee venom to treat various ailments, most importantly arthritis."

"That's right!" came a voice from the end of the table. "As a child, I used to watch my aunt go into her garden, catch a bee, and let it sting her arm. She said it helped her arthritis."

"Well, there are a lot of people experimenting with bee venom as a treatment for arthritis. It's called apitherapy. Up in Middlebury, Vermont, a beekeeper named Charles Mraz administers bee venom to people suffering from arthritis. There was an article about it a couple of years ago in *Country Journal*. According to the article, he isn't accused of practicing medicine without a license, because he uses bees to administer the venom and he doesn't charge patients. Now I'm not saying that bee venom will work for everyone. There are certainly enough beekeepers who have arthritis in spite of being repeatedly stung. Also the U.S. medical establishment is skeptical about bee venom as a treatment for arthritis. Nevertheless, doctors acknowledge that there haven't been sufficient studies. In Europe especially, they are continuing to look into bee-venom therapy.

"The trouble with most doctors, in my opinion, is that they spend too much time worrying people about the harmful effects of bee venom. Now I'm not suggesting that you're not allergic to bees," I said, pointing my spoon across the table again, "it's just that nearly everyone is being told they are. About the only people who aren't allergic these days are beekeepers. When I get stung, it still burns at the moment the sting goes in, but there is no swelling afterward. In the spring, when I haven't been stung all winter, there is a little swelling, but by the end of the summer I'm immune.

"Most people when they get stung, say, by walking barefoot in clover, have a localized reaction. There's a swelling and soreness near the sting. That's not an allergy.

"What everyone should worry about are those very few cases in which a sting is followed by shock, unconsciousness, and death.

"But such a serious reaction is incredibly rare. In the whole United States there are only forty deaths a year from bee, wasp, yellow jacket, and hornet stings combined. That makes these insects slightly more dangerous than snakes, which kill fifteen people per year, but virtually harmless compared to cars, which kill fifty thousand.

"At Harvard there is an allergist named Dr. Howard Rubenstein who thinks doctors are scaring people unnecessarily about bee stings. He claims that there is no evidence to support the belief that there is a predictable progression from simple localized reaction after one sting, through generalized itching and hives, breathing difficulties, and abdominal cramps, to death after subsequent stings. In fact, there are many cases in which people have died from a bee sting without apparently ever having been stung before. There are also people who have had difficulty breathing after one sting and had a much milder reaction after the next."

I had hoped that the woman across from me would be relieved by this news. She didn't seem to be.

"Among the causes of the forty deaths that occur each year, Dr. Rubenstein suspects that, in addition to some genuine allergic responses, there are also heart attacks, toxic reactions to the venom itself, and fear. Some people, convinced by their doctors that they are allergic, probably just die of fright.

"Now, fear is a perfectly real thing. If you're afraid of bees (for whatever reason), you should carry a bee kit with you that has antihistamine in it and epinephrine hydrochloride. But as Dr. Rubenstein says, most people need to be protected not so much from bees as from alarmist propaganda."

The woman across from me got up from the table. "That's fascinating," she said. "I simply had no idea bees could be so interesting. How did you ever manage to learn all that? I'll be lucky to remember half of it if I'm ever bitten again."

12

A DRINK
YOU CAN SWIM
IN

Water has become a fashionable drink. At clubs, bars, the most gala receptions, it is *de rigueur* to stand about holding a glass containing nothing stronger than ice, water, and a slice of lime. But the water that is being sipped doesn't come from the faucet. It's being poured from bottles, more than 500 million gallons last year alone. Water, with no calories, no artificial sweeteners, no caffeine, is the essence of lightness, the drink of the elite, the elegant, the sophisticated, or so the advertisements whisper. Samuel Clemens, who observed that to increase something's popularity you have only to increase the price, would smile to learn that while city tap water costs about a tenth of a cent a gallon, a gallon of bottled water is selling for $5.

Whether you are rich or poor, whether you drink water out of choice or necessity, the attention that has been devoted to the bottled variety is a reminder that all waters are not alike. Bottled water is being judged with the same concentration and articulation used in wine tasting. Consumers Union convened a panel of taste experts to judge thirty-six kinds of bottled water. "Excellent water," the experts explained in the September 1980 issue of *Consumer Reports*, "should be clear: free of sediment and color. Its aroma should be clean: free of obvious off-odors such as those of chemicals or manure. An excellent water's flavor should also be clean, though it may stimulate just slightly the tastebuds that sense sweetness, bitterness or sourness. But most of all, an excellent water should be refreshing."

These experts were drinking water by the glassful, a common enough way to judge its quality, but not the only way. Millions of other people have been testing the water all summer long. Instead of merely raising a glass of water to their lips, they first remove all or most of their clothes. Then, after slowly (or rapidly) immersing their entire body, they swim.

Sipping water while seated at a table is simply no match for swimming. There is no comparison between swirling a sample of water around the inside of a glass and swirling yourself around the inside of a sample of water. A swimmer cannot escape the odor of the water; at most, it is inches from one's nose. To judge its clarity and color, you have only to look down. To taste it, open your mouth and an unlimited draught will flow in.

Those people who never drink while they swim have spent too long in the ocean or in chlorinated pools. Fresh water is meant to be drunk, and anyone who has ever been thirsty, desperately thirsty, delights in the knowledge that even the most gargantuan drink will not drain a lake.

Ask swimmers which kind of water they prefer to swim in and most will say a lake, one that is deep and clear, with nothing floating on the surface and only rock or sand on the bottom.

Choosing a lake is more complicated than choosing a brand of bottled water. Lakes come in all sizes and shapes, of different depths and different ages. Some have streams flowing into them, others are spring-fed. The most common way of classifying them, however, is in terms of their productivity—the amount of organic matter that is produced per square meter per year. Swimmers, whether they realize it or not, are looking for an oligotrophic lake. Oligotrophic means poorly fed, and an oligotrophic lake has a low concentration of plant nutrients in its water. With few nutrients, there are few plants. Such lakes are most likely to be deep and clear with a sandy bottom.

Nutrient levels in a lake are hard to measure, but there is a simple device for measuring clarity, called a Secchi disk. Named after Pietro Angelo Secchi, an Italian astronomer, the disk apparently originated with Commander Cialdi, head of the Papal Navy, who conducted a series of experiments with Professor Secchi on board the S.S. *Immaculate Conception* in 1865. Simple enough for any swimmer to use, the Secchi disk is a white disk 8 inches in diameter that is lowered into the water on a string. The clearer the lake, the farther down the disk can be seen. In most oligotrophic lakes, the Secchi disk can be seen at a depth of 20 feet or more. In Crater Lake in Oregon, which is 1,932 feet deep, the disk has been seen at depths of 131 feet.

There was a time when it was easy to find an oligo-trophic lake. Most lakes in the northern United States were formed by glaciers, which scoured out basins in the native rock, or piled up dams of glacial debris, or left behind big buried blocks of ice that ultimately melted and created kettles like Walden Pond. Shortly after the last glacier re-ceded, there were oligotrophic lakes all across the country—deep, clear, clean-water lakes, all with bare bottoms. But that was 10,000 years ago.

To see what difference a hundred centuries can make, you must realize that even the clearest lake is not sterile. There are things growing in it. Suspended in the water is phytoplankton—minute plants, such as diatoms, desmids, and filamentous green algae—which requires sunlight for photosynthesis. The phytoplankton is being eaten by zoo-plankton—equally minute animals, with names like rotifer, copepod, and cladoceran. They, in turn, are being eaten by nekton, those larger, free-swimming animals that include aquatic insects and fish.

As pure as an oligotrophic lake may seem, it is actually a dilute broth, and, like a broth on which a layer of fat is floating, the water in a lake is stratified. Any swimmer who has dived toward the bottom of a lake has discovered that there is a much colder layer of water a short way down. This is the hypolimnion, a layer of cold—and hence heavy—water on which floats the lighter, warmer water of the epilimnion. Between the two layers there is a zone of rapid temperature change called the thermocline. During the summer, there is very little mixing of the layers. In the fall, when the surface water cools, it sinks to the bottom, carry-ing its dissolved oxygen with it, and the bottom water, car-rying nutrients, is displaced to the surface. A similar turnover of the lake water occurs in the spring when the ice melts.

Turnovers of the lake, in which nutrients are carried to the well-illuminated surface waters, are often accompanied by a proliferation of phytoplankton. During the summer, many of the zooplankton migrate vertically, moving to the surface once a day to feed and then settling back to the depths. Largemouth bass and muskellunge also live in the food-rich epilimnion. Lake trout, however, move deeper into the cold hypolimnion as the summer progresses.

Although there is a long list of things that live in oligotrophic lakes, the water is not crowded. In fact, there is virtually no chance that a mouthful will contain anything detectable. But while the creatures in an oligotrophic lake have little effect on swimming conditions during their life, their death is another matter.

As they die, their remains drift to the bottom, there to contribute to the bottom ooze, an organic muck where bloodworms and phantom midges survive on what little oxygen is left after decomposition. This muck builds up very slowly, about a millimeter a year, but after 10,000 years, the rain of tiny corpses may have resulted in 30 feet or more of sediment. In a lake that was hundreds of feet deep originally, this probably will have no effect on the water quality, from a swimmer's point of view. Provided there is a large volume of water deeper than plants can grow, the lake will remain in something of a steady state.

However, some lakes are shallow to begin with, and when sediment has further decreased the depth, much more of the lake bottom will be shallow enough for rooted plants to grow. What was once only a fringe of rushes and sedges around the edge becomes broad expanses of pickerelweed, arrowheads, and cattails. The rest of the lake's surface may be plastered over with waterlily pads. Such a large amount of aquatic vegetation consumes equally large amounts of oxygen as it decomposes. This high biological oxygen demand, as it is called, depletes the oxygen in the hypolimnion and trout can no longer live in the lake. Instead, perch, pike, bass, panfish, and bullheads become the dominant fish. Eventually, as sedimentation continues century after century, the lake will fill in altogether, becoming first a marsh or swamp and then a forest.

When lakes change from deep, relatively unproductive ones to shallow, highly productive ones, the process is called eutrophication. Lakes at an intermediate stage are called mesotrophic, and because of their well-developed fish populations, many mesotrophic lakes are very popular. The progression of lakes from oligotrophic to eutrophic doesn't always occur the same way, but when a lake does fill in it is perfectly natural—natural and incredibly slow. Immeasurably slow from the point of view of an individual swimmer. Find a lake that is still oligotrophic and from the perspective of a human life span it will remain oligotrophic indefinitely—deep, clear, clean, inviting. Or at least that's the way it should remain.

Oligotrophic lakes, however, attract swimmers the way a bare arm attracts mosquitoes, and many of the best swimming lakes have gone through the following stages of human colonization:

The first summer, a tent is pitched on the shore of a wild and deserted lake. Next year, the tent acquires a platform, and since word has got out about how clear the lake is, how fine the swimming, the tent has acquired neighbors. Before long, the tent platforms have evolved into the floors of small cottages. Since there are too many people in the summer community to "go around behind a bush," outhouses are constructed. In short order, these are replaced by indoor toilets. The toilets, in turn, are connected to cesspools made by filling 50-gallon steel drums with rocks.

As long as the community remains a summer one, the water in the lake remains as clear and as clean as it was when first discovered. But summer communities have a tendency to change into year-round ones. Roads are paved for winter use. Drains are dug and culverts are laid. The trees surrounding the lake are cut down and grass seed is sown. Businesses are established, so that residents won't have so far to commute. The cottages all around the lake are themselves improved: roofs are raised, furnaces put in, dishwashers and washing machines installed. But one thing stays the same, the 50-gallon drums filled with rocks, the drums by now very rusty and the rocks coated with grease.

The human body produces about 10 pounds of nitrogen and 1.3 pounds of phosphorus in the form of sewage every year. Homeowners who wash with detergents containing phosphates can double the phosphorus content of their waste water. Both nitrogen and phosphorus are essential plant nutrients. In fact, the growth of plants is usually limited by the availability of these nutrients, especially by the availability of phosphorus. Letting nitrogen and phosphorus drain into a lake is like spreading fertilizer on a garden. It causes the lake to bloom.

The bloom, a population explosion of algae, is not a pretty sight. Swimmers, the first to detect a change in the water quality, don't need a Secchi disk to tell that the water is cloudy. They can no longer see their own feet. What was once clear all summer long is now a pea-green murk by July. What's more, the water tastes funny and smells bad.

The nutrients flowing into the lake aren't just from the homes on the lake's perimeter. Lakes are low points in a landscape, and the nutrients come from wherever water flows toward the lake. This area of drainage, or watershed, as it is called, extends from the lake shore to the tops of the nearest mountains. Street drains carry lawn fertilizer and waste from thoughtfully curbed dogs. The smoke from coal and oil furnaces contains significant amounts of nitrates, and these may be washed down in rains. In the more rural parts of the watershed, the runoff carries manure from horses, cows, and other livestock. Here and there, a town sewer or a pump on a sewer line is leaking raw sewage.

The more of this that reaches the lake, the more the water deteriorates. Large mats of blue green algae appear on the lake surface and are blown onto the beaches by on-shore winds, where they look like human excrement and smell worse. Lakefront residents may end up closing their windows, perferring the heat to the stench. As unpleasant as the algae is to people, it's worse for the fish. The more algae, the more oxygen needed to decompose it when it dies and the less oxygen available for fish to breathe. Ultimately, even the carp, the last species in the lake, are gulping air from the surface. Soon they too are asphyxiated and float belly up, as the entire epilimnion of the lake becomes anaerobic.

What has happened to this once oligotrophic lake is that it too has become eutrophic, and in a period of only years or decades, not centuries. Furthermore, the lake has reached its state of high productivity by a very different route from natural eutrophication. Natural eutrophication is the result of gradual filling of a lake with sediment. This artificial enrichment of a lake produces a similar outcome but is called cultural eutrophication to reflect the fact that it is associated with the activities of humans. Cultural eutrophication is not an isolated occurrence. The National Eutrophication Survey, conducted by the Environmental Protection Agency from 1971 to 1977, looked at 800 lakes receiving municipal waste water and found that 68 percent were eutrophic.

Just because the water in a lake is green, tastes bad, and smells funny doesn't stop some people from swimming in it. It's probably a good thing that people don't drink very much water when they swim or a lot more of them would get sick from swimming in culturally eutrophied lakes, for mixed in with the plant nutrients there are usually plenty of bacteria. As it is, many bathers contract "swimmer's ear" and "summer diarrhea," the former a staphylococcus infection of the outer ear, the latter a coliform bacteria infection in the gut.

The public-health hazard of a polluted lake is too often overlooked until something serious happens. Perhaps a number of people contract a more serious waterborne disease or someone goes under for the third time and rescuers can't find the body in the green murk. Then the Public Health Department, which has been reluctant to shut down a recreation area, formally closes the lake to swimming, citing coliform counts greater than 2,000 per 100 milliliters, or Secchi disk readings of less than four feet.

Long before the lake is a public-health hazard, however, it is an eyesore, not to mention a pain in the nose. The lake that was once the raison d'être for the community has become its bête noire. Lakefront residents storm into selectmen's meetings and demand that something be done. In response to such pressure a number of things have been tried.

Copper sulfate, spread in judicious amounts, kills algae without harming fish or aquatic invertebrates. From 1926 to 1936, between 60,000 and 100,000 pounds of copper sulfate were applied annually to Lake Monona in Madison, Wisconsin. The result was copper-rich layers of sediment on the bottom of the lake and an annual reappearance of the algae. Whether copper sulfate is used or one of the modern biodegradable algicides, there will be no lasting benefit unless the flow of nutrients into the lake is stopped.

The same is true of efforts to restock a lake. Fishermen lamenting the passage of trout may demand that the town rid the lake of carp and other "trash" fish and restock. Rotenone, the familiar garden insecticide, is spread on the lake, and since fish are exquisitely sensitive to the chemical, which blocks their respiration, they all die. Trying to introduce trout into such a lake, however, is a waste of fingerlings, for unless the biological oxygen demand has been reduced and oxygen has been restored to the cold hypolimnion, they will die, just as surely as if they themselves had been given rotenone.

Cultural eutrophication can be reversed, a fact that also distinguishes it from natural eutrophication, which is essentially irreversible. However, reversal requires that the entire watershed be treated, not just the lake itself. The improvement in the water quality of the lake will not be as instantaneous as poisoning all the algae, but in the long run, treating sources of lake degradation rather than the byproduct is more cost-effective.

Finding where the excess nutrients are coming from can be as simple as noting where the storm drains empty. Septic-system seepage is harder to locate. Tracking the path of household waste is made easier by flushing a dye down the toilet. Sometimes the dyes show up immediately. Even if they don't, they can be detected in laboratory analysis of lake water.

Identifying pollution sources is only the first step. Stopping them is another. It requires understanding, public concern, and money. Lots of money. If the lake offers public access, some of the money comes from the state and federal governments. Ultimately, however, lake restoration depends, not on Washington, but on local landowners and officials, on lakefront associations, conservation groups, and sportsmen's clubs. There are still plenty of culturally eutrophied lakes that need improvement. But gradually watersheds are being improved, the destructive flow of nutrients into lakes is being halted.

Once the flow of nutrients to a lake has been halted, it makes sense to begin restoration of the lake itself. Lakes with large enough streams flowing in and out of them may have enough water exchange to make in-lake treatments unnecessary. In some lakes it takes only a few days to replace the water. In Lake Superior it takes a few centuries. In a closed, spring-fed lake with no outlet, the phosphorus content of the water may remain high and continue to promote the growth of algae for a very long time. Spreading aluminum sulfate in the lake will incapacitate the phosphorus by binding with it to produce an insoluble compound that settles to the bottom.

Stands of larger aquatic vegetation can be destroyed

with herbicides. If chemical control is objectionable, mechanical harvesters can be used. These harvesters are usually self-propelled floating machines that mow or uproot submerged plants.

Another way to destroy vegetation along the shore is to lower the level of the lake with pumps and allow the weeds in shallow water to dry out or freeze depending on the season. Called "drawdown," the lowering of a lake's level also makes it easier to dredge sediment from the bottom. Dredging, however, is controversial. If the sediments are contaminated with toxic chemicals, they may be more dangerous on land than at the bottom of the lake. Simply stirring up the bottom sediment may resuspend herbicides, pesticides, and industrial wastes and reintroduce them into the food chain of the lake.

Then there is biological control, whereby species are introduced to the lake to control the growth of plants automatically. Eutrophic lakes have been experimentally stocked with a variety of organisms, from algae-eating water fleas to water hyacinth-consuming manatees. Although the use of predators rather than poisons to keep the water clear is attractive, exactly how to do it remains to be worked out.

Knowing how to restore lakes is one thing, but deciding what to restore them to is quite another. Obviously, it is impossible to return every lake to its postglacial origins. The Federal Water Pollution Control Act Amendments of 1972 set some national goals, specifying 1983 as the year in which all water in the United States should be swimmable and 1985 as the year by which all discharge of water pollutants will be halted. Swimmable doesn't mean oligotrophic.

It simply means safe, and even that goal won't be realized on schedule. There is talk of "accepted levels for projected use," words that sound like an excuse to do nothing, to claim that since a lake is too disgusting to swim in, no one will want to anyway.

Lake restoration is expensive. Installing new sewage-treatment plants is very expensive. But any method is going to be expensive. It's a matter of deciding what to spend one's money on. At $5 a gallon, the dollars being spent for bottled water would buy a lot of lake restoration.

Deciding which lakes will be restored and to what level they will be restored will require a community consensus involving not just the lakefront residents but all those who live in the watershed and all those beyond who ever have or ever might enjoy the lake's water. In the end, the decisions will involve almost everyone, for a third of the nation's population lives less than 5 miles from some publicly owned lake and 99.4 percent live within an hour's drive.

From all the debate over which lakes to restore, a simple suggestion emerges—a sort of "grandfather clause" for lake restoration. If the lake was oligotrophic when your grandfather swam in it two generations ago, then it should be made oligotrophic once more. The water should be deep and clear—clear enough to see the bottom all year-round—and clean—clean enough to drink with impunity. No, not just impunity. One should be able to float in the middle of millions of gallons of water and drink one's fill with the same enthusiasm bestowed upon the finest bottled import. The first person in the lake each summer should be able to call back, "Come on in, the water's fine"—and mean it.

13

TRACKSIDE

Saint Louis, Missouri. Gateway to the West, a 630-foot-high stainless-steel arch. Lewis and Clark, Charles Lindbergh. Birthplace of T. S. Eliot, home of the Cardinals. Gaslight Square, Washington University, and two big botanical gardens.

Yes, two. Everybody knows one of them, the Missouri Botanical Garden on Tower Grove Avenue, with its giant geodesic-dome greenhouse, the Climatron. The other botanical garden occupies more land, but scarcely anyone, including residents of Saint Louis, knows that it exists. It's open seven days a week. There's no admission fee, you can walk on the grass, and the management lets you pick flowers.

I shouldn't be publicizing my new discovery, especially in print. Publicity usually results in hordes of people descending on a place and ruining it, but this second botanical garden is already accustomed to a lot of traffic. It's located along the railroads in Saint Louis, the right-of-ways, the freight and switching yards, the sidings. Saint Louis has the second largest railroad network in the United States, second only to Chicago. At the edges of yards, around the buffers at the ends of sidings, in the sand, gravel, cinders, and crushed stone that make up the ballast in which the crossties are bedded, there are plants. Most of them look like weeds, most of them *are* weeds, and even the largest have none of the attractiveness of the palms, bromeliads, and African tulip trees in the geodesic dome called the Climatron. Yet to a degree, the freight and switching yards can be called a botanical garden, or so I have learned from Viktor Muhlenbach.

Viktor Muhlenbach is an employee of the Missouri Botanical Gardens, but his real allegiance is to railroad flora. Even before coming to this country, he spent 20 years studying the plants along the railroads of his native city, Riga, Latvia, and he has been walking the tracks of Saint Louis since 1954. The results from 563 of these latter excursions have recently been published in the *Annals of the Missouri Botanical Garden* under the title "Contributions to the Synanthropic (Adventive) Flora of the Railroads in St. Louis, Missouri, U.S.A."

The case for calling the freight and switching yards a botanical garden rests on the kinds of plants that are found there. Along railroads, Muhlenbach reports, "one may find a multitude of rare, strange, and unfamiliar plants." His article describes 393 species, none of which are native to Missouri and many of which had not been recorded previously, such as *Potentilla argentea*, the silvery cinquefoil from Eurasia, or *Verbena brasiliensis* from South America. Most of the species are weeds, not native but widespread: Japanese honeysuckle (*Lonicera japonica*) from Asia, creeping bellflower (*Campanula rapunculoides*) from Europe, castor bean (*Ricinus communis*) from Africa, and Dallis grass (*Paspalum dilatatum*) from South America.

You expect to find ailanthus and marijuana along the tracks, for they are symbolic of waste places, but Muhlenbach also found onions and garlic, sesame, coriander, and dill. On his walks he came across numerous peach trees, some apples, an apricot, and a pear. Asparagus was widespread, along with beans and corn. Cucumbers, melons, and squashes were present, but rare. He found amaranthuses, larkspurs, petunias, roses of Sharon, snapdragons, and a lot of weeds (which Muhlenbach, the botanist, treated with equal enthusiasm). One is left with the impression that the railways are a richly varied garden, weeds and all, but lest one assume that there is a profusion of fruits and vegetables ripe for the taking, it should be noted that the strawberry plants Muhlenbach found were sterile, the beet had a remarkably thin root, and the peaches were of inferior quality.

What is so remarkable about the plants growing along the tracks is that they are growing there at all. They weren't planted. Unlike botanical gardens, where introductions are intentional and careful records are kept, the plants along the railways thrive unanticipated and unnoticed. How, then, did they get there? Railroads, it turns out, are particularly good at dispersing seeds, a fact that was noted shortly after the first railroad with steam traction was inaugurated in England in 1825. Wherever tracks were laid, unfamiliar plants began to appear.

The majority of seeds travel on freight trains. Shipments of grain, for example, often contain smaller weed seeds, and these sift to the bottom of the cars as they bump along, eventually falling off the car on curves or in the switching or classification yards where cars repeatedly jolt together. Hay or straw used as packing material may also contain seeds, and when the cars are emptied on cleanout tracks, the seeds are discarded with the refuse. Cattle being moved by train carry seeds with them, as do the trailers riding piggyback on flatcars. The freight cars themselves may pick up hitchhikers. Muhlenbach examined several freight cars and found seeds stuck to the lubricating cups of wheels and in the runners of the sliding doors. Even railroad workers inadvertently carry seeds. Muhlenbach examined the clothing of a switching crew in the North Saint Louis Freight Yard and found a great many seeds in their cuffs.

While most seeds travel by freight, high-speed passenger trains may transport lightweight seeds in the vortex of air they create behind them. Other seeds, in the form of wilted flowers and apple cores, may be tossed out the windows. Tomato seeds may reach the track by yet another route, one remembered in the song:

> *Passengers will please refrain*
> *From flushing toilets while the train*
> *Is standing in the station.*
> *I love you.*

Finally, railroad tracks are perceived by many as a convenient place to dump rubbish of all sorts, refuse from adjoining residences and surrounding neighborhoods. The squashes and pansies came from someone's garden waste, the grape hyacinths from lawnmower clippings.

Not only are the plants along the railroad track accidentals, but every attempt is made to eradicate them. In the past, this was done by hand, but now chemical herbicides are applied with devastating success. "For the most part, they are doomed," says Muhlenbach, describing the fate of his discoveries. The trend toward replacing the top layer of ballast with coarse stone or gravel is also reducing the numbers of plants, since seeds cannot germinate in it. Remodeled tracks, he laments, are often desolate throughout.

Even if a plant gains a foothold and escapes the weed-control crew, it is subject to a host of disasters. A specimen of *Rumex dentatus*, the first plant of the species to be discovered in Missouri, was smothered by rubbish in 1970, and the whole area was bulldozed a year later. A colony of toad-flax (*Kickxia elatine*) that had persisted for sixteen years was destroyed by a spill of lubricants and paint. A colony of burdock (*Arctium minus*) was buried by the wreckage of a derailed freight train.

One-quarter of the introduced species that Muhlenbach recorded, he saw only once. Wiped out by climate or misfortune, these species are constantly being replaced by others. Some actually become tenuously established. But while some colonies flourish, other thriving populations disappear. Blue mustard (*Chorispora tenella*), which had been a rarity up until then, suddenly developed a huge colony, while a colony of butter-and-eggs (*Linaria vulgaris*), which had grown in a very secure locality for eight years, suddenly vanished.

Viktor Muhlenbach's enthusiasm for walking along railroads may seem somewhat unusual, but it is essentially the same enthusiasm that gets bird-watchers out of bed before dawn or sends beachcombers down to the shore. None of them know beforehand what they will find. The excitement of encountering a new plant is the same as that of spotting an accidental bird, perhaps a migratory species blown off course by a storm. It is also the thrill of discovering a message in a bottle washed ashore by the tide. Such excursions are risky, of course. There is always the chance that you'll find nothing, but that chance makes the findings more momentous. Beyond noting that railroads, winds, and waves do move things from place to place, there is no certainty, no guarantee of what will happen when. That very uncertainty is more important than most of us realize. God does play dice with the universe, and out of the uncertainty comes anticipation, and, in turn, hope. In Saint Louis, more than gamblers frequent the tracks.

14

SOPHISTICATED FLYPAPER

In the kitchen, several nights ago, my wife was telling me about the marriages of fifteenth-century Italians while I was finishing the peach pie left over from dinner. She had gotten to where the bride is lifted off the ground and carried bodily to the altar, when a cockroach walked out from behind the sink and proceeded across the drainboard. It wasn't one of those little roaches, the Oriental or German ones. It was a big American roach, reddish brown with two long antennae that it kept waving about. My wife explained that the custom of lifting the bride was to acknowledge her reluctance to wed, and with her bare fist she bashed the cockroach to a pulp. Then while continuing to talk about marriage, she reached for a paper towel, wiped up the splatter of guts and broken exoskeleton, cleaned off her hand, and tossed the whole mess into the trash under the sink.

I can't do that. Call me spineless, but I don't even like the crunchy sound that cockroaches make when you use your foot. Don't get me wrong, I'm not at all keen on the germs the roaches are spreading around the kitchen. Unfortunately, I'm even less keen on the method most commonly used to stop them: spreading poisons around the kitchen. It's easiest to just hope that the roaches will go away. At other times, I find myself similarly hoping that houseflies will go away, and yellow jackets, and mosquitoes, and Japanese beetles, indeed a great variety of troublesome insects.

It doesn't work, of course, this hoping that troublesome insects will leave you alone. Huddled beneath the sheet you can hope heartily, you can wish willfully, you can shout "Bug off" through the percale, and the mosquito will continue to circle hungrily in the warm updraft of your body odor until you emerge and give blood.

When not dining on us, insects are feeding on our livestock and our crops, eating our houses and the trees that shade them. Faced with sometimes devastating losses, people have prayed, fasted, and sacrificed in an effort to make the insects go away. They have shouted, beaten drums, waved their arms, sticks, pieces of cloth. All for naught.

In the Middle Ages, Europeans went so far as to conduct trials of insects accused of damaging crops. Courts issued extradition orders, and if insects failed to leave the country by the time specified in these orders, the insects were threatened with malediction and excommunication. By the sixteenth century, this method of insect control had become very exact: the Burgundian lawyer Bartholomaeus Chasseneux (1480–1542) wrote an entire treatise on the rules for bringing suit against grasshoppers. Unfortunately, the combined power of church and court was no more effective than wishful thinking. Following a suit against cutworms in 1497 in Berne, Switzerland, in which the cutworms were declared guilty, excommunicated by the archbishop, and banished, a contemporary writer noted that "No effect whatsoever resulted," and attributed the failure to "the great depravity of the people."

While higher authorities were busy banishing insects from the realm, individuals were trying to save their own skins with a variety of insect repellents. If a substance was offensive enough, it was believed to repel insects. So people spread pitch and tar on themselves, and sprinkled their clothes with camel urine. Offensive they must have been. The twentieth century brought better protection from mosquitoes, flies, gnats, and their various cousins and relations: citronella oil (1901), dimethyl phthalate (1929), Indalone (1937), and Rutgers 612 (1939). The large number of soldiers stationed overseas during World War II prompted a search for an even better repellent, one that was nontoxic, nonirritating, nonplasticizing, and long-lasting. To date the best is diethyl toluamide, DEET, the principal ingredient in nearly all insect repellents. Yet as everyone knows, even the best bug dope deters the ravenous beasts for only a short while. And now some researchers are privately warning that insect repellents may be harmful to the user's health.

From all of this there emerges a single conclusion: personal, legal, ecclesiastical, or chemical, no matter what kind of stink you make the insects won't go away. We have been wasting all this energy trying to drive insects away when we should have been trying to attract them instead. Many insects can be lured into a trap and disposed of neatly. I like this idea much more than bashing them one by one, or waging war with insecticides, both of which seem equally heavy-handed.

There is no record of who first thought of attracting insects. Lucius Junius Moderatus Columella, a first-century Roman, recommended hanging fish in trees to attract ants. However, he also claimed you could protect the garden from caterpillars by nailing up crayfish in various places, or by having a woman, ungirded, with her hair flying, run around the place barefoot. Japanese peasants who once relied on torchlight processions and prayer to drive off insects noticed, by the Middle Ages, that fires actually attracted and killed some of them. In the eighteenth century, European women had slender metal cylinders suspended from cords about their necks. Fleas prancing about milady's bosom could enter the cylinders through small holes, but they became trapped on a smaller sticky tube inside. Nineteenth-century winegrowers baited traps with molasses and wine lees to catch vine moths. And as long as any of us can remember there has been flypaper.

Lately, however, the use of insect traps has become more and more widespread. The most conspicuous ones are the fluorescent blacklight traps. Reminiscent of the psychedelic generation, these traps glow nightly in restaurant parking lots, on driving ranges, and in suburban backyards. The traps exploit the attractiveness of light, especially ultraviolet light, for night-flying insects. The insects spiral into the bulb and wind up fried on an electric grid, drowned in water, or imprisoned.

Other traps that are visually attractive to insects are not as easy to recognize at first. The sticky, red croquet balls hung from the branches of fruiting apple trees are attracting and catching adult apple maggot flies whose larvae are responsible for the brown tunnels in apples. The equally sticky yellow squares in a greenhouse filled with tomato plants are trapping whiteflies which suck plant sap. Shake an infested tomato plant, says one of the trap's designers, Ralph Webb of the U.S. Department of Agriculture, and "most of the whiteflies will fly to the cards like iron filings to a magnet." The sticky, white plywood pyramids on top of metal fence posts in a field of cattle are trapping face flies; the sticky sheets of white cardboard nailed to telephone poles are trapping the beetles that spread Dutch elm disease.

As in the familiar flypaper, stickiness is an active ingredient of many insect traps. A coating of heavy motor oil (SAE 90) will hold tiny insects like whiteflies, but it is not sticky enough for larger ones. Wardle and Buckle's 1923 *Principles of Insect Control* lists eight recipes for adhesive, among them "resin, 3 parts; cottonseed oil, 1 part," and "Venice turpentine, 1; American Turpentine, 4; castor oil, 2." Most traps today, however, use one of several commercially available sticky materials that go by such names as Tack Trap, Tanglefoot, and Stikem. These are soluble in mineral spirits, but are generally unaffected by rain or extreme heat or cold.

There are sticky traps that even catch roaches. In 1973 Earth Chemical of Japan introduced Gokiburi Hoy-Hoy

("Hey, Hey, cockroaches, come over to my house"), a full-color, gaily decorated box, 7 inches long and 2 inches high, with a sticky floor that fatally mired any roaches that ventured inside. In this country the popular Roach Motel from Black Flag is one of several copies of the Japanese design. A little larger than a cigarette pack with an entrance at each end, the Roach Motel also contains a food-scented bait. From a distance one sees only an inconspicuous, white, unmarked box. Most Americans are more uptight than my wife about roaches in the kitchen.

If you are feeling frugal you can make your own roach traps from pint jars. Smear the top 2 inches inside the rim with petroleum jelly and set them upright where you suspect roaches. Slices of apple or potato placed in the bottom of the jar will lure American roaches, while bread or banana will lure German roaches. The live roaches caught in the bottom of the jar can be drowned in hot soapy water.

Whole food baits are, of course, not practical for commercially manufactured traps, so there has been much screening of chemicals in search of the odor that a particular insect finds most attractive. Octyl butyrate, an ingredient in synthetic fruit flavorings, and geraniol, principally used in perfumes, will attract yellow jackets and Japanese beetles respectively. Tsetse flies are drawn to carbon dioxide bubbled through acetone, a scent that researchers in Zimbabwe have labeled "synthetic cow's breath."

Far more attractive than any of these food scents, however, are a class of chemicals produced by the insects themselves called pheromones. Many of these help one sex to find the other, and as a bait in a trap, they not only attract the prey from a great distance, but they are extremely species specific. One difficulty with a blacklight trap is that on a warm summer's night 2 quarts of insects may be caught, most of them not the pest species. A pheromone-baited trap, on the other hand, will catch almost nothing but the pest species. Once it was necessary to imprison a virgin female in a trap to produce the attractive chemical; now a couple of hundred pheromones have been isolated, identified, and synthesized.

The Health-Chem Gypsy Moth Trap looks like a milk carton with a porch roof going all the way around to shield the entrance ports. The bait inside is a laminated polymer: the middle layer containing the gypsy moth sex pheromone disparlure (*cis*)-7,8-epoxy-2-methyloctadecane and outer layers of the sandwich controlling the evaporation, so that the bait gives off a steady scent. A male moth emerging from late June to September zigzags upwind toward the trap, confident that he is homing in on a virgin female. He enters the trap, and still searching for the siren that has called him, dies, the victim of a dose of insecticide.

All these traps work. That is, they all catch insects. But do they catch enough to make any difference? It may be emotionally satisfying to revenge yourself by killing a roach or two, but this hardly makes a dent on the number in the kitchen. Can insect traps be used for control? It depends.

There have been some real success stories. Ronald Prokopy, now at the University of Massachusetts, Amherst, set out 469 of the sticky red spheres in 81 fruiting apple trees in his orchard in Wisconsin. Female apple maggot flies seeking an apple in which to lay an egg and male flies seeking a female with which to mate both flew to the dark red spheres and stuck there. In all, the balls captured 9,689 apple maggot flies, enough that the percentages of apples infested by apple maggots was only 1.1 to 2.7 in the three kinds of apples in the orchard, compared to the 97.2 and 98.2 percent in the unsprayed control orchards.

There have also been some real busts. Those blacklight traps, the ones with the electric grids that crackle, spit, and pop when insects hit them, are supposed to be controlling mosquitoes. The advertisements say they do. A close look at the dead insects will reveal that a great many non-mosquitoes are being killed, but this might be dismissed as a fair price to pay if the traps produced a mosquito-free outdoors. However, as two Ontario scientists, G. A. Surgeoner and B. V. Helson, have recently demonstrated, there are just as many mosquitoes biting in backyards equipped with an electrocutor as in ones without.

Most insect traps fall somewhere in between. For traps to control the population of an insect pest, you usually have to set out a lot of them. In 1980, the Swiss set out 20,000 sticky yellow panels in cherry orchards to control cherry fruit fly. The Israelis used 450,000 such traps to control olive fruit fly. The Swedes and Norwegians in a cooperative program set out nearly a million pheromone traps to catch bark beetles killing Norway firs.

If there is a high density of insects, pheromone traps often fail because of competition between the trap and natural sources of the pheromone. Health-Chem's Dr. Agis Kydonieus is quick to say, "If you have a million gypsy moths per acre, the traps won't work. For big infestations you use BT (*Bacillus thuringiensis*), a biological insecticide, or chemical insecticides, and then traps." Furthermore, if the pheromone traps lure only males, as many do, you have to catch all the males or the remaining ones will impregnate the females. Even if all these difficulties are overcome, there may still be totally unanticipated problems, such as the one Dr. Louis Roth of the Army Quartermaster Corps found when he was experimenting with B-periplanone, a sex pheromone of the American cockroach that attracts males. "We discovered that some of the eggs of *Periplaneta americana* can develop without being fertilized. Although the number of nymphs that hatch from unfertilized eggs is low and the number that reach maturity is small, all individuals that become adults are females, and they too can reproduce without mating." Dr. Roth is as frightened by the prospect of a race of parthenogenetic roaches as I am.

When you ask entomologists, most are skeptical that traps will ever control more than a few species of insects. But once again, as with the discovery that insects won't go away, this is not such bad news. Just because a trap won't control a pest directly doesn't mean it won't help control pests indirectly. A trap that is worthless for control may be superb for monitoring, which is determining whether or not a particular pest is present, and if so, in what abundance. Monitoring is the basis for a promising new method of insect control called Integrated Pest Management.

In the past, insecticides were applied quite indiscriminately, often in anticipation of a pest's appearance. This only produced resistant strains and new pest species. Now increasingly used in concert with biological and cultural controls, insecticides are being applied only when absolutely necessary. Insect traps, used for monitoring, are helping entomologists, farmers, foresters, and exterminators determine when that is.

In New England, the corn earworm, a fat caterpillar

that burrows into and feeds on the ends of ears of corn, cannot survive the winter. Each summer the grayish brown adult moths spread north searching for corn silk on which to lay their eggs. To track their progress, farmers now place a single 15-watt black-light bulb as close as possible to freshly silking sweet corn. The trap is examined three times each week, and the grower holds off applying any insecticide to his corn until the first corn earworm moths are caught. Even then the frequency of subsequent applications will depend on how many moths are caught.

For monitoring traps to provide comparable information from year to year and from place to place, they must stay the same. Changing the number of traps set out, the position of the trap, the attractants, or the design of the trap will affect the numbers caught. Therefore, a number of standard sticky traps have been designed, generally pieces of sticky paperboard to which the appropriate pheromone bait can be attached.

Inventors will, of course, continue to search for a simple, inexpensive trap that will control insects by itself. The rest of us will pin our hopes on trap-based Integrated Pest Management. Neither control nor management means eradication. The ancestors of cockroaches were here 300 million years before us, and their descendants will be here years after. We should have realized this all along: as unwelcome as some insects are, we're stuck with them.

15

ILL WINDS

"Pollinosis, seasonal rhinitis, summer catarrh," I hear
the breeze whisper like some secretive offering from
a darkened doorway of a Middle Eastern bazaar. I could turn
away, but instead I allow myself to be overcome, breathing
deeply of the intoxicating air, willingly, for I am immune.

It is difficult to be eloquent about hay fever. Difficult
to compose fine phrases about inflamed mucous membranes, sneezing, eyes that itch, and a nose that runs. I can't
even draw on personal experience, for I am, as I said, immune. My companions who suffer through the aestival rites
offer me little help. They are all speaking rather nasally
and pitifully between plies of the handkerchief.

Until recently I viewed hay fever as a troublesome and
silly ailment visited upon others, millions of others to be

sure, but nothing that I had to take a personal interest in. And then I happened to read an essay by E. B. White written for *Harper's Magazine* in July 1938. White, a sufferer from the early type of summer catarrh, is recuperating on his farm in Maine, as he expresses an inspiring enthusiasm for hay fever. "I find in this strange sensitivity to male dust and earth's fertile attitude a compensatory feeling—a special identification with life's high mystery which in some measure indemnifies us for the violence and humiliation of our comic distress."

This male dust, of which White speaks so glowingly, is pollen, the essential half partner in the sex life of plants. For years the odor of roses was blamed for the summer torment of the membranes, and the affliction was called rose fever or rose cold. The nineteenth century deserves the thanks of rose fanciers, first for renaming the disease hay fever, then suggesting grass pollen as a cause, and finally for proving it a little over a century ago.

The failure to implicate pollen at once is perfectly understandable. Pollen is so small it's scarcely distinguishable and at the same time so common it appears omnipresent. The grains of pumpkin pollen, some of the largest, are still only 200 microns in diameter. At the other extreme are the grains of forget-me-not pollen—scarcely 4.5 microns in diameter. How could anything as inconspicuous as pollen be responsible for wreaking such nasal havoc? Three hundred years ago, people hadn't deduced that pollen was the progenitor of seeds, let alone a runny nose.

It required the invention of the microscope before people could get a good look. Nehemiah Grew of England and Marcello Malpighi of Italy share the honor of being first to scrutinize pollen. In 1682 Grew published his findings:

The Particles of these powders, though like those of Meal or Dust, they appear not easily to have any regular shape; yet upon strict observation, especially with the assistance of an indifferent Glass, it doth appear, that they are a Congeries, usually of so many perfect Globes or Globulets; sometimes of other Figure, but always regular. That which obscures their Figure is their being so small: In Dogs-Mercury, Borage, and very many other Plants, they are extremely so. In Mallows, and some others, more fairly visible.

. . . Those in Snap-dragon, are of the smallest size I have seen; being no bigger through a good Microscope, than the least Cheese-Mite to the naked Eye. In Plantain, also through a Glass, like a Scurvy-grass-Seed. In Bears-foot, like a Mustard-seed. In Carnation like a Turnip-seed. In Bind-weed like a Pepper-Corn. In all these of a Globular Figure.

In Devils-bit, they are also round, but depressed, like the seed of Goose-grass, or a Holland cheese. In the Bean and all sorts of Puls, and Trefoyls, also in Blew-bottle, &c. they are Cylindrick. In Orange Lilly, Oval, one 5th of an Inch long, like an Ants-Egg. In Deadly-Nightshade, also Oval, but smaller at both Ends. And those of Pancy, Cubick. In all these and the former, they are Smooth.

But in Mallow, Holyoak, and all that Kind, they are beset round about with little Thorns; whereby each looks like the Seed-Ball of Roman Nettle, or like the Fruit of Thorn-Apple, or the Fish called Piscis arbis minor, or the Murices, used anciently in Wars.

Today pollen is described as having a tough outer coat, the exine, surrounding a thin inner sac, the intine, which in turn surrounds two or three cell nuclei. The exine, sometimes decorated with spines, knobs, or other protrusions, also has characteristic furrows that allow it to stretch as the pollen grain absorbs moisture. These furrows also have germinal pores, from one of which a pollen tube appears when the pollen germinates after landing on a stigma. This pollen tube, which in corn may be 10 inches long, grows until it reaches the ovule. Two nuclei will pass down this tube on their way to fertilizing the egg and creating the endosperm.

Before this can occur, however, the pollen must travel from the anther where it has been produced to the stigma atop the ovary. In beans it only needs to travel a fraction of an inch, but for hollies the distance may be half a mile.

Such flowers as dandelions, apple blossoms, and asters have come to rely on insects to transport their pollen, which is sticky or has long spines. In orchids or milkweed blossoms, the pollen is conveniently packed in carry-out bundles called pollinia. This type of flower uses colorful petals to attract pollinators, scent as an added incentive, and nectar as a reward. Never mind that some such flowers are pollinated by birds, bats, mice, and other noninsects, the flowers are all generally termed entomophilous, or insect loving.

A second group of plants called anemophilous, or wind loving, rely on air instead of animals. The oaks, the grasses, and the ragweeds have dispensed with petals and perfume. Their pollen lacks spines and has no tendency to stick together. Designed to ride the smallest air current, the grains tend to be between 17 and 58 microns in diameter. Larger grains would fall too rapidly. Curiously, the smallest pollen grains are also insect dispersed, perhaps because their proportionately greater surface area causes them to stick together.

It's important to recognize the difference between entomophilous and anemophilous pollen: the latter is the villain in hay fever. There are, of course, rare exceptions. A florist who spends days emasculating lily blossoms so they will last longer, or anyone else who spends unusual amounts of time fiddling with anthers, could become allergic to entomophilous pollen. However, for pollen to become an important cause of respiratory allergy like hay fever, it must be contained in the air we breathe. From the earliest catkins of willows to the last stand of ragweed before the frost, the air is thick with male dust. Not that most of us notice it. We continue to breathe normally, blithely unaware of any hazard.

A few of the populace, however, immediately detect that something is adrift. When a few pollen grains are drawn into their noses and dissolve in the mucous, allergens penetrate the tissue and quickly complex with immunoglobulin antibodies causing the release of such chemicals as histamines. These in turn cause a dilation of the capillaries, a contraction of the nasal muscle, a hypersecretion of nasal fluids—in short, a hay fever attack.

Wine tasters, tea judges, and other gourmets may boast about the sensitivity of their noses. But these cannot compare with the sensitivity of a hay fever nose. Not that everyone is sensitive to every wind-borne pollen. Many people are specialists, and their suffering is confined to the few days or weeks when their particular species of antagonist is airborne. Even those whose beaks are aquiver from March to

October cannot claim the distinction of total sensitivity.

If you are allergic to one species of grass such as Kentucky bluegrass (*Poa pratensis*), you may be allergic to others as well. However, just because you are allergic to black-oak pollen (*Quercus nigra*), you are not necessarily allergic to white-oak pollen (*Q. alba*). Cross-sensitivity is very difficult to predict.

Allergists spend many office hours testing new patients to see what they are allergic to. The skin test involves scratching or injecting separate pollen extracts, each made from a different species, into the skin. The degree of redness, itching, pain, or any wheal that appears defines whether or not the patient is allergic to the pollen being administered.

Other tests involve inhaling the pollen extract and measuring nasal drip, or sending a sample of the patient's blood to a lab where it is directly mixed with various pollen extracts in order to see if allergic antibodies are present.

Learning which pollen is responsible for one's hay fever provides little relief. Finding the anther just isn't enough. For many people, relief is best obtained with antihistamines, carefully selected so that the dosage doesn't make one drowsy.

For the most serious sufferers there is injection therapy involving weekly shots of pollen extracts administered well before the pollen season begins, so that the patient is immune by the time the first pollen appears in the air. Unfortunately, the shots rarely confer permanent immunity. They are slightly painful and, at $100 per year for the materials alone, expensive.

Enough people suffer from hay fever that the demand

for allergenic extracts, both for testing and therapy, supports a dozen companies who harvest pollen from 400 to 500 species of plants.

There are three methods used to collect anemophilous pollen. One is water-setting, which involves cutting stems of plants before the pollen is released and placing them in water surrounded by clean sheets of paper onto which the pollen falls.

A second method is to go over flowers outdoors with a vacuum, but this requires a pure stand, and even then the sample may be contaminated with other wind-borne pollens.

The third method, and the least satisfactory, is to macerate the entire flower and separate out the pollen.

Virtually all of the pollen collected is anemophilous pollen, but doctors can also buy extracts of rose pollen, perhaps to convince stubborn patients that they aren't suffering from rose fever. For the gardener who blames the flower garden, there are extracts of pollen from such other entomophilous species as aster, chrysanthemum, sunflower, and zinnia.

While many of the companies have their own staff of collectors, they still employ a hardy band of independent pollen harvesters. Curiously, the cash value of the collected pollen has remained very stable. Thirty years ago collectors were paid $1.50 a gram for poplar pollen. Today they are paid $1.50 to $1.75.

Increased federal regulation of the pollen harvest threatens to drive prices upward and to restrict the number of species collected, but business is booming. Elizabeth White, director of Greer Laboratories in North Carolina, one of the suppliers of allergenic extracts, estimates that collectors are being paid from $2 to $3 million this year. At least someone besides the allergists is benefiting from an ill wind.

It is too bad that the pollen gathered by these collectors does not result in a cheap and painless cure for hay fever. For while a "shot in the arm" is a popular metaphor, that's all that is popular about it. I may never have had an attack of hay fever, but I can't imagine that even the worst symptoms would make a battery of hypodermic injections seem attractive. I think I'd side with those who believe eating pollen cures the disease. Carlson Wade's *Bee Pollen and Your Health* (1978) says: "By taking one teaspoon of bee pollen daily, resistance to wind-carried pollen is slowly built up, and sensitivity to allergy is reduced. Gradually your body builds up a shield to insulate you from the irritating effects of wind-carried pollen." Since the pollen that most people are allergic to is wind-dispersed pollen, it's not clear why bee pollen should provide any immunity. "To help build a form of natural immunity your body requires a supply of entomophilous pollen," says Wade. I can see that a honeybee body needs a supply of entomophilous pollen, but why the human body? If bee pollen is ever proved to provide immunity to hay fever, it may be due to some cross-sensitivity between anemophilous and entomophilous pollens, or a few grains of wind-dispersed pollen contaminating the bee pollen.

You can't read about bee pollen without encountering all sorts of diseases reputedly cured by eating it. The list reads like a medical encyclopedia: acne, arthritis, asthma, burns, colds, diabetes, flu, hay fever, menopause, prostatitis, radiation sickness, rheumatism. Criticism leveled at airborne pollen is drowned out by acclaim for the bee-borne variety—the miracle food.

One thing I'm sure of is that bee pollen is good for bees. A tenth of a gram is all it takes to raise a bee from egg to adult. Pollen added to the feed ration of hens increased laying 17 percent in the first 60 days over a control group receiving a balanced diet complete in vitamins and micronutrients. Also the egg yolks were reportedly a more desirable yellow. Beyond birds and bees I'm unwilling to back claims for pollen's efficacy in the diet. I don't doubt that it's nutritious, but when it comes to miracle foods, I'm a confirmed agnostic.

Amateurs are encouraged to experiment with bee pollen because it is so easy to collect. The bees do most of the work. A pollen trap consisting of a screen and a container is fitted over the entrance to the hive, and when returning workers crawl through, the screen dislodges the pollen balls being carried in the pollen baskets of the bees' hind legs. The container catches the falling pollen.

Royden Brown harvests an estimated 65 pounds a year from each of his hives, and his C. C. Pollen Company of Scottsdale, Arizona, sells more than a million pounds a year. Because it's easier to collect, bee pollen is cheaper than the pollen collected for the preparation of allergenic extracts, but it isn't cheap. The smallest amount Brown sells is $40 worth. That gets you 3 pounds 10 ounces of his Arizona High Desert Honeybee Pollen. Other companies sell it in smaller quantities, but the price per ounce makes it an expensive food.

Being healthy has a number of disadvantages. One of them is that you don't get to say yes to a long list of doctors' queries. The other is that you are a poor subject for testing miracle foods. Nevertheless, I went out and bought a single ounce of "100% Pure Bee Pollen." An investment of eighty-nine cents. In addition to the aforementioned medical problems, bee pollen is said to reduce anxiety, stress, and fatigue—conditions to which I confess a slight predisposition. I figured it also wouldn't hurt to get a head start on longevity and continued potency.

The pollen is in small pellets, about half the size of Grape-nuts cereal, that are all yellow but with the same variation in hue as red barns. The texture is slightly chewy, and there is a sweet taste that comes from the regurgitated nectar the bees have mixed in while molding the pellet. I couldn't think of how to describe its taste, until someone suggested, after accepting a sample, that it tasted like a blend of poppy seeds and sulfur.

They told me at the health food store not to expect immediate results. They seemed to be sure of that. They were a little less sure of what results I should be expecting. I've got my fingers crossed about one thing, and I'll let you know at the first sign of an improvement. There's an enormous market and a fortune to be made if bee pollen proves to be a cure for writer's cramp.

16

---◆---

FAIR DAYS FOR
VEGETABLES

People who don't fish grow tomatoes. It gives them
something to brag about. Tomatoes are better than
trout in this regard, for in addition to size and number,
there is the matter of earliness. In our town, people try to
have ripe tomatoes by the Fourth of July, scarcely a month
after the last frost. The first one, usually rather diminutive
and still somewhat orange, may be picked June 30 and is
cause for public proclamation. Preseason trout, on the
other hand, are illegal and not much discussed.

Over a ham-and-bean supper in the town hall, people
speak glowingly of their tomatoes, each report bettering the
preceding one until tomatoes sound as plentiful as trout at
a fish hatchery. By the sound of it, everyone had fresh tomatoes along with their salmon, green peas, and fireworks.

But gardeners will no more admit to being skunked on opening day than will fishermen. The fact is that the July tomatoes, so publicly proclaimed, must have been privately eaten, because native tomatoes didn't start showing up at potluck suppers until August.

The most competent tomato growers won't rise to the bait of postprandial exaggeration. If asked, they will point out that there is only one crop of tomatoes a year and that quality is more important than earliness. The eating quality of the earliest tomatoes, 'Sub-Arctic Early', for instance, is only acceptable, a taste that falls far short of what people expect from a homegrown tomato. Who has the best tomatoes this year is a question that doesn't really get resolved until the second weekend in September, at the Hillsborough County Agricultural Fair.

The tomatoes start arriving on Thursday, the day before the fair opens. Each has been individually wrapped in tissue paper, towels, or newsprint, and nestled in shallow boxes. Mindful of potholes and thank-you-ma'ams, the drivers of the pickup trucks and VWs have taken their time getting to the huge horse barn on the fairgrounds in New Boston, New Hampshire. There, scores of exhibitors unpack their entries, arranging them on white paper plates, which in turn are set out on long trestle tables. Except for requests to pass the entry tags, no one says much. Some people have typed their tags out in advance, but most are writing their names and addresses and "Class 23, Division 3," which is tomatoes, and under that, 'Burpee's Big Boy', 'Marglobe', 'Roma', 'Rutgers', 'Sweet 100', or 'Heinz 1350'.

Tomatoes aren't the only vegetables being exhibited. Heads of celery, cabbage, and cauliflower appear along with parsnips, pickling cucumbers, and Brussels sprouts. 'Mammoth Russian' sunflower stalks are brought in and entered as the tallest plant or the largest head. Half-pints of dried beans are set out along with containers of fresh herbs. Pairs of men stagger past holding up the ends of feed sacks on which lie huge pumpkins. Watermelons nearly as large belie the fact that at this latitude the end of the growing season is about two weeks away. Even with everything packed close together, the 1,500 vegetable entries are enough to cover five of the 75-foot-long tables. By 10 o'clock, when the barn doors are rolled shut for the night, everything has been unpacked and the empty boxes are hidden away under the tables.

Rules for exhibiting vegetables seldom get written down. The Premium List published by the directors of the fair specifies only the quantities: "Division 3. Five each of the following: Beets, Carrots, Radishes, Onions, Parsnips, Sweet Corn, Pop Corn, Ornamental Corn, Tomatoes (ripe or green), Gourds, Potatoes." It adds that "tops of root vegetables should be removed 1½ inches above vegetable; corn to be exhibited with only one side of the husk removed." More than that the new competitor must learn from experience or by talking with others.

Amateur tomato growers accustomed to superlatives such as earliest or largest are unprepared for the emphasis on uniformity, the insistence of the judges that all five tomatoes be identical in size, shape, color, and ripeness. Vegetable exhibits have never been intended as sideshows for the display of freaks, but rather as demonstrations of the expertise of the gardener. The tomatoes should give the impression that all one's tomatoes look like these five. This isn't true, of course. Most exhibitors have been saving every tomato that ripened in the last ten days and are exhibiting only their best.

The current record holder for the largest single tomato is Clarence Dailey of Monona, Wisconsin, who grew a 6-pound, 8-ounce tomato in 1976. But unless he had four others the same size, he couldn't have shown it at New Boston. There's a big difference between growing the world's heaviest tomato and exhibiting a perfectly matched set of five—the difference between weight lifting and gymnastics. In the future, someone in Tucson or Hackensack will grow a bigger tomato and Clarence Dailey's record will be shattered. But beautiful plates of tomatoes appear every year in New Boston, and each year they are compared to each other, not to last year's or those in the next county.

In addition to uniformity, prize-winning tomatoes must be blemish-free—no cracks, no blossom-end rot, no catfacing, no green shoulders, no brown spots, no thumbprints. Already "unshippable" as far as commercial growers are concerned, a ripe tomato is so subject to trauma that it must be handled with great care.

If a tomato is supposed to be small, like 'Small Fry' or 'Tiny Tim', then exhibiting small fruit is fine; but 'Delicious' tomatoes are supposed to be large, a pound or more apiece. This is called trueness to type and means that the exhibit should reflect the description of the tomato in the seed catalog.

Finally, judges look for something that is called "eatability." It is a given that all the tomatoes being exhibited taste good, for there is no vegetable that stands so clearly above its store-bought counterpart as the homegrown tomato. But even here there are degrees of perfection. The tomatoes should not be underripe, but neither should they be overripe. You shouldn't have to cut into it to taste it. The feel against one's hand, the luster of the skin, the almost overpowering tomato musk, should be enough.

These, combined with a certain artistry in arranging the tomatoes on the plate, are the sorts of things that judges take into consideration when choosing the best five of each kind of tomato that makes the trip to the fair. Actually, more than five tomatoes make the trip. A sixth or seventh is included as insurance. Everyone takes out insurance on green tomatoes. They ought to be easy enough to exhibit, but according to rules (again, unwritten) they must be full-size green tomatoes. One of these always turns pink, if not on the way to the fair, then between the time the doors close and the judges arrive in the morning.

The vegetables are on the far side of the fairground. To get there once the fair has opened, one must pass through the midway. Sallow young men and women shaking their change belts urge the optimistic, the proud, the gullible to test their skill, try their luck, win a snake for the lady. Screams from the Ferris wheel mix with smoke from the chicken barbecue. Jack's French Fries, Angie's Pizza, Big D's Sausage Subs. Carve your sign, draw your portrait, paint your face. Get your kraut dogs, foot-long hot dogs, steamed hot dogs, Creed's cheese. Up on the hill, teams of oxen are dragging a wooden sledge loaded with concrete as a loudspeaker announces the results of the last hitch. Tacos, fried dough, salad-in-a-pouch, blue Sno-Kones. The New Hampshire Fair's Queen walks by in a white satin gown, her silver pumps sinking into the sand and coarse gravel; her escort wears jeans. Cotton candy and steak sandwiches. In the horse ring, 4-H girls under eighteen canter their horses, attracting more attention in their tight jodhpurs than the band playing on the stage. The air is thick with dust, the smells of food and livestock, the clanging of horseshoes, the baas of market lambs led into the ring by their chins. A uniformed state trooper stands under the pines at the information booth, the symmetry of his face broken by a huge plug of chewing tobacco.

It is darker and cooler in the horse barn, where the vegetables are, and quieter, too. The board-and-batten building has plastic panels in its aluminum roof that let light down on a third of an acre of sandy floor. Some of the space is used for exhibits of rabbits, poultry, maple syrup, garden tractors, chain saws, Hammond organs, and political parties that either want to build more nuclear power plants or do away with them altogether.

But the vegetables are the center of attention, even more colorful now that they are spattered with ribbons. There are hundreds of blue and red ribbons and an occasional yellow one. The entries have been judged on the Danish System: 90 to 100 percent quality is Grade A and gets a blue ribbon; 80 to 89 percent quality a red Grade B; 70 to 79 percent quality an ignominious yellow Grade C. The yellow ribbons go mostly to new exhibitors who haven't yet learned not to exhibit a zucchini that looks like a snake swallowing a rabbit.

In the aisles, people are crowded together as close as the plates on the table—families have come from Concord, Manchester, Nashua, all the way from Boston. This is not one of those fairs where the public is separated from the vegetables by a barrier of chicken wire like some old-fashioned zoo. While parents momentarily hold up a 'Lemon' cucumber or read the entry tag on a 'Tahitian' squash, smaller hands reaching up from below the edge of the table may make off with a 'Yellow Plum' tomato or two. But Everett Upton is there to prevent the exhibition from turning into a pick-your-own operation. Though he's missing all his lower teeth and has to sit down now and again, Everett Upton is still Vegetable Superintendent, a job he has held for ten years. He enters vegetables himself, but you won't find his name on any of the entry tags. He enters them in the name of the woman who drives him to the fair, figuring that she might as well get a little money back for her time and gas.

It won't be much money. An "A" ribbon only brings seventy-five cents, a "B" fifty cents, a "C" a quarter. There is a sweepstakes contest with five rosettes going to the five competitors who have won the most blue ribbons, but first prize is only $15. There are $50 worth of premiums for the largest watermelon, money contributed by Ben Hogan, an organic farmer from Nashua. But Ben Hogan and his family have a tendency to win it back with watermelons weighing 51, 52, 53, 63 pounds—in a state that developed 'New Hampshire Midget' supposedly so that the natives would be successful growing watermelons in such a short season.

If exhibiting vegetables in New Boston is not a money-making proposition, it is a friendly rivalry, with stakes too low to generate much passion. People faithfully return year after year to see if they can win the sweepstakes, to see if they can fool the judges by pinning the broken stem back on an albino acorn squash, to show everybody that they can produce winning tomatoes year after year. They come with vegetables, but much of their real reason for being there is to visit one another. This is a once-a-year meeting for many. They come to New Boston almost expecting to see Fletcher Wason, tall, gentlemanly, slightly hard of hearing, who carried a paper cup to spit in, who grew a dozen kinds of potatoes, who didn't plant bush beans until six weeks before the fair, who won second prize in the sweepstakes every year, and who would still be exhibiting if he hadn't bent over to fix a chair rung while putting on his shoes and quietly died. To say hello to old Mr. Merrill, dressed in his best purple suit, the cuffs rolled, a paper poppy in his wide lapel, whose pride is an American chestnut tree still bearing fruit. His only entry is a peck-basketful of the sea-urchin-like burrs. To talk with Richard Hechtl, who spends his winters teaching psychology, his summers managing an enormous garden and an equally enormous family, who once sorted through an entire bushel of crab apples to find five good ones, who more than anyone else has grown the best tomatoes in every color from pink 'Ponderosa' to orange 'Jubilee' and ivory 'White Beauty'. The exhibitors at the Hillsborough County Fair spend much of their weekend standing around admiring each other's handiwork, answering questions ("No, ma'am, that's kohlrabi").

There is no fence between the vegetable exhibits and the public in New Boston, because the people who exhibit the vegetables are no different from those who come to see them. They both spend a lot of time talking about tomatoes. This may once have been an unintentional side effect of everyone's growing tomatoes, but no longer. Now people are growing tomatoes, at least in part, because it provides them with something to talk about. (Similarly, most people who go fishing don't do it just because they like the taste of trout.) No other vegetable doubles as a social passport, no other vegetable makes it so easy for people of different ages, incomes, and educations to talk to one another. For many, just the subject of tomatoes is enough to leave a good taste in their mouths.

17

SEVEN STEPS
TO A
BETTER BOUNCE

The cleaned fruit then passes into a sorting machine where each berry is given seven chances to bounce over a four-inch barrier. Berries that fail are discarded.

Step One

Few people can name six native North American food crops. Corn isn't one. Neither is the potato nor the tomato. All three originated in the Andes. However, the pecan and the sunflower are from North America, as are the fox grape and the Jerusalem artichoke. And two fruits in the genus *Vaccinium*, the blueberry and the cranberry.

Called *sassamanesh, atoqua, a'-nibi-bim,* and *ibimi* by the Narraganset, Algonquin, Chippewa, and Leni-Lenape Indians respectively, cranberries were mixed with dried meat and fat to make pemmican. The Pilgrims, who renamed the fruit because they fancied its flowers resembled a crane's head, also ate cranberries, but there is no proof that they did so at the first Thanksgiving. In 1703, cranberries were served at the commencement dinner at Harvard College, and in 1816, Henry Hall transplanted some wild vines into a swampy spot in Dennis, Massachusetts, to establish the first domesticated bog. Thus came *Vaccinium macrocarpon* into cultivation.

Step Two

Cranberries need an acid soil, an abundance of water, and a moderately cool summer. Living in bogs and swamps, the evergreen plant produces trailing woody stems up to 6 feet long, from which rise 2- to 3-inch uprights that bear pinkish white flowers and the globular red fruit.

In building a new cranberry bog, a natural bog is first drained by cutting a ditch all the way around it. The grasses, sedges, sphagnum moss, and Labrador tea are stripped off with a bulldozer or dragline. The material from this scalping can be used to build dikes, and the level peat surface that remains is then covered with 3 inches of coarse sand.

Unrooted cranberry cuttings 6 to 8 inches long are simply stuck into the sand a foot or so apart. It takes three years for the vines to cover the ground and bear even a half harvest. In the interim, however, they must be protected from mosses, ferns, horsetails, sedges, grasses, and a host of broadleaf weeds, against all of which cranberries are poor competitors. The young vines must also be protected from fungi that cause tip blight, red leaf spot, red gall, and fairy rings. The blunt-nosed cranberry leafhopper will spread the virus disease that causes false blossom. The black-headed fireworm feeds on terminal leaves, making bogs look as though a fire had swept through them.

If this isn't enough to discourage the would-be cranberry grower, the bog must be flooded every winter to prevent winterkill. Enough water is let in through a dike from a reservoir to cover the vines. When the surface has frozen, the remaining water beneath the ice is drained out, leaving a blanket of ice over the vines. Flooding is also used to prevent late spring frosts from damaging the vines, but a sprinkler irrigation system is superior for this, since it requires much less water. Once the bog is bearing, every few years additional sand, perhaps half an inch every three years, is spread on the bog, usually in the fall or winter. This smothers some of the weeds and gives the cranberry vines more soil in which to root.

It's not surprising that the cultivation of cranberries is very limited. In the United States the principal cranberry-producing states, from the largest to the smallest, are Massachusetts, Wisconsin, New Jersey, Washington, and Oregon. In Canada, British Columbia, Nova Scotia, New Brunswick, and Prince Edward Island produce cranberries. In all, this adds up to only about 25,000 acres of cranberries, and there seems little likelihood that the United States acreage will ever increase dramatically. Except in Oregon, where cranberries are being grown in sand with extensive irrigation, cranberries are grown on bogland, and further development of such land soon runs into restrictions, regulations, or protests from some government agency or conservation group. In Canada, where by law no more than 3 feet of peat may be mined from a peat bog, people are looking around for ways to use stripped bogs. Some of them are turning to cranberries, and Canadian acreage may indeed increase. But for most growers, increased harvests will not come from more land, but from higher yields on the existing acreage.

Step Three

Between 75 and 100 days after bees have pollinated the blossoms, the cranberry fruit matures. The fruit is too small to pick one at a time; it takes 90 to 130 'Early Black' cranberries just to fill a cup. For centuries the solution was a hand-held wooden scoop with long pointed tines. The tines were slid under the berries and the scoop rocked backward to dislodge the fruits from the vine. With one of these a skilled picker could harvest a barrel of cranberries (100 pounds) an hour. Today hand scoops are still used to glean the edges of ditches, but many more are used as magazine racks and planters.

One of the first mechanical cranberry pickers was developed after World War II by Thomas Darlington, a grower in New Lisbon, New Jersey. Resembling a gasoline-powered lawn sweeper, the Darlington machine is still widely used in eastern bogs. Rows of metal teeth revolve in front, stripping the berries from the vines and passing them to a conveyor belt, which drops them into a box held between the handlebars. With a mechanical harvester a person can pick cranberries ten to fifteen times faster than someone with a scoop—as much as an acre a day. Dry harvesting, as the technique is called, is used when the berries are to be sold fresh, for the berries are dry and unbruised. However, the machines miss a good percentage of the fruit, 20 to 30 percent if the bog isn't perfectly level.

For this reason most cranberry bogs are now wet harvested. Tiny red flags are set out to mark the location of the ditches, and the bogs are flooded. Since cranberries have an airspace in the fruit, the fruit floats. A machine called an eggbeater, or a water reel, churns up and down the bogs, its twin reels frothing the water and dislodging the fruit. From a distance the mass of floating fruit looks like a bloom of red duckweed on a shallow lake. The floating berries are corralled by a boom of linked two-by-fours and towed to the side of a dike where an elevator lifts them out of the water, removes the dead leaves, and dumps them in the back of an idling tractor trailer.

Partly as a result of switching over to wet harvesting, which not only harvests more fruit but is less punishing to the vines, the yields of cranberry bogs have been increasing. The average harvest is 100 barrels per acre, but some growers consistently harvest 250 to 300 barrels per acre. Massachusetts, in 1971, was the first state to harvest a million-barrel crop and broke this record again in 1978 and 1979, on about 3,800 fewer acres than thirty years ago.

Step Four

Asking for cranberry juice when someone offers you a drink sounds more sophisticated than ginger ale, and the bartender's eyebrows don't go quite as high. You can sip the zero-proof drink slowly and give the impression that it contains alcohol. Even if you forget and gulp it too rapidly, you will only lose your sophistication, not your ability to focus or balance.

Stores still sell cranberry sauce and cranberry jelly, but two-thirds of the 2.6 million barrels of cranberries harvested last year became juice. Frozen first to make them easier to process, as well as to improve their flavor and increase their juice yield, the cranberries are then mixed with rice hulls to make them easier to press. The ruby liquid that flows out of the presses is too sour to be popular, so high-fructose corn syrup is added. Ocean Spray, a 700-grower national cooperative that processed 2.2 million barrels of last year's crop, sells cranberry juice as Cranberry Juice Cocktail, correctly identified in smaller type as "a juice drink." There is no artificial coloring added to the cranberry juice, and on the back of the Ocean Spray label is a note that says, "The color of Ocean Spray Cranberry Juice Cocktail may vary slightly according to the variation in the natural color of cranberries." A lot of effort is devoted to keeping that variation to a minimum. At the Ocean Spray processing plants, separate batches of juice are stored in separate tanks and then blended according to their degree of redness to achieve a uniform product. Nevertheless, there are bad years—1979 was one of them—when the whole harvest is of a poor color.

There's a lot of talk about wonderful future uses for cranberries. A veterinarian discovers that cranberry pulp can be used as a cattle feed. A professor of food-process engineering at MIT announces that cranberry sponge—the residue left after pressing—traps more than fifty times its weight in water and can be used as a food thickener or to produce natural juiciness in fabricated foods. A food technologist at the American Institute of Baking reports that a cranberry concentrate outscored the banned Red Dye No. 2 as an effective food coloring.

But all the pulp produced in Massachusetts would only

be enough to feed two average-size New England dairy herds. Use of cranberry sponge or a cranberry concentrate would first require FDA approval and would have to prove to be economically superior to existing alternatives. And besides, who needs new ways to use cranberries. The demand is for juice. Five years ago surplus cranberries were being dumped in the woods. Today 52 percent of American households drink cranberry juice, and the demand is so great that there aren't enough cranberries to meet it.

Step Five

The Massachusetts Cranberry Festival and 4-H Fair is held each fall on the grounds of the Edaville Railroad, a steam train that takes passengers on a circuitous tour of the pine woods and cranberry bogs of South Carver. Amid antique autos, jugglers, wood-carving demonstrations, a pony-pulling contest, and a bluegrass band stands a tent full of cranberries. Inside they are giving away cranberry juice, and a lady is showing you how to make cranberry-orange relish with a food processor. At one end they have set up a screening demonstration. Boxes of freshly harvested cranberries are being poured into a separator, where the berries fall onto the first of the wooden slats. If the cranberry fails to bounce over the adjoining barrier, it falls to the next board, and so on, until it bounces or is discarded. The good cranberries then run along a belt beside which several women sit and pick out any unripe or bruised fruit that have gotten through. There's a booth for the National Cranberry Quilt Patch Contest and a long table covered with the day's entries in the Cranberry Baking Contest.

The women in the tent are volunteers belonging to an organization they call the Cranberry Connection. "We're all wives, mothers, daughters, sisters, or sweethearts of cranberry growers," says Jean Gibbs, whose husband, Philip, raises cranberries on 30 acres of his own and on another 30 acres that belong to his mother. The Cranberry Connection was created in the early seventies when a group of Plymouth County women were trying to interest the nonfarming community in a farmland assessment bill. The first few years they held an Open House on the Cranberry Bog and a tour of the Ocean Spray Processing Plant at Middleboro. But since the unpredictable New England weather makes an open house in the open somewhat risky, the women were glad to move to a tent at the Cranberry Festival.

The group, now thirty to forty strong, is principally concerned with persuading people to use fresh cranberries. They aren't opposed to people drinking juice, but as Jean Gibbs explains, "Those of us who have been growers for a long time feel that if we wiped out fresh fruit it would be a detriment to the industry. Besides," she adds, "with all this worry about what goes into food, if you have your own fresh cranberries, you can do what you want with them."

The Cranberry Baking Contest is one way to encourage people to cook with cranberries, and this year I've been asked to help with the judging. I'm enthusiastic. Never having judged anything besides flowers, vegetables, and bunny rabbits, I don't know how to judge food, but it's nearly lunchtime and I am ravenous with enthusiasm. Besides, I will only be assisting Jean O'Connell, who is a bona fide food editor from the Springfield *Republican*.

The breads are the hardest to judge, but a few loaves are overdone, a few are underdone, and a few more don't have enough cranberries in them. In the end the blue ribbon goes to Amerine Thorburn of Halifax, for a competent although unoriginal bread. All of the loaves have been sampled.

There is a wider selection of pies, a cranberry mincemeat and a mock cherry. The winner is a cranberry cheese pie made from cranberry-orange relish and cream cheese by Charlene Lawson of Carver. It is clear who the front-runners were; there are great wedges of pie pan showing.

The professional judge, I tell myself, does not gorge on the early entries. It dulls the palate, and besides, one might become too sated to enjoy a later entry that is truly magnificent and demands further sampling.

This proves to be the case, for in the "any other imaginative way" class are No-Bake Cranberry Peach Treats by Marlene Resnick of Kingston. It would be quibbling to ask what a no-bake item is doing in a baking contest. Her Treats are small tarts, made by covering the bottoms of six aluminum foil cupcake papers with chopped almonds. Then comes a second layer, made by blending ½ cup ricotta cheese with ½ cup cottage cheese, and adding maple syrup to taste. On top of this is a third layer, made by boiling together for 15 minutes, one cup of cranberries and one cup of peeled, chopped, fresh peaches, with more maple syrup added to taste.

A recipe high in calories, high in price, and high on my list of favorite desserts. I was too busy polishing off the tarts to note that all three winners—Marlene, Charlene, and Amerine—had names that rhymed. We left a couple of tarts because it didn't seem proper to have a Best of Show ribbon on an empty plate.

Step Six

Ripe; ripe and fresh; dark red beauties; nature's rubies. Fresh; fresh and plump; flavor and health. Tangy; toothsome; tart and tempting. These are the words and phrases that sell cranberries, printed on the plastic bags of fresh fruit, splashed across the front windows of grocery stores.

But there's more to marketing than coining phrases like "bog-born bonanza." Ocean Spray's New York public relations firm, Creamer Dickson Basford, has been promoting cranberry as a color. It's the first time, they claim, that a color has been used to sell food. Fifty fashion designers were invited to designate cranberry as a fall color. A goodly number from Adolfo to Vera Maxwell went along with the idea. A similar invitation was delivered to furniture designers. At High Point Market in North Carolina where the furniture makers convene, they gave away cranberry juice and T-shirts that said Everything's Coming Up Cranberry. Meanwhile, the public relations firm was scouring Europe for chefs, eventually selecting nine from England, France, Belgium, Italy, Sweden, and Japan. All were persuaded to develop recipes using cranberries.

The culmination of this was a show staged in the windows of Sloane's furniture store in New York City, in the fall of 1979. Cranberry-colored clothes and furniture were displayed along with three of the chefs demonstrating their cooking to passersby. The show was repeated in stores across the country.

Is the promotion effective? "We think it's working," says Creamer Dickson Basford, "and Ocean Spray seems to be pleased with it." Just as Kansas City has learned to eat lobster, a taste for cranberry will soon extend far beyond the plant's natural range. In advertising jargon, "product acceptance" is spreading—to the American Southwest, to Sweden. Kikkoman, the soy sauce company, has become the Japanese distributor for Ocean Spray, and one Japanese television station even sent a camera crew to photograph an American woman using cranberries in her own kitchen.

Step Seven

"To further expand the market, new types of cranberries may be developed which can be eaten raw and whole. This is one of the few fruits that may be eaten in theater, movies, etc., as it is not juicy and has no peel or core." Just think how much easier it would be to clean up after the show. All the spilled cranberries would be down in the front row. No shells, no butter—very wholesome—a bit too wholesome, perhaps, until children learn that a cranberry can also be a weapon.

Irving Demoranville and F. B. Chandler proposed the above idea twenty years ago. I called the Cranberry Station in East Wareham, Massachusetts, to see what had happened since 1960. Demoranville, now the Extension Cranberry Specialist, chuckled and said, "The project just died on the vine."

While it may be only a small loss for Saturday matinees, the fate of the project seems to reflect a general disinterest in cranberry breeding. Four cultivars account for some 85 percent of the harvest, and all four were discovered in the wild before 1900: 'Howes' from Bassett Swamp in East Dennis, Massachusetts, 1843; 'Early Black' from a swamp in Harwich, 1852; 'McFarlin' from New Meadows bog in South Carver, 1874; and 'Searles' from a swampy brush patch in Walker, Wisconsin, 1893.

Of the more than a hundred named cultivars, some were named for the town where they were first planted: 'Berlin' (Wisconsin), 'Holliston' and 'Centerville' (Massachusetts). 'Early Ohio', however, grew in Wisconsin. Other cultivars were named for their discoverers: 'Atwood', 'Early Richard', and 'Perry Red'. A cranberry discovered by J. F. Stankiewicz seems to have become 'Stankavich'. On Martha's Vineyard, Albert Berry's find was called 'Berry Berry', suggesting that the island had a vitamin deficiency.

These cultivars, however, all came from wild seedlings —the offspring of chance hybridizations. They were discovered in the wild and subsequently propagated. Not until 1929 was there any controlled breeding. H. F. Bain and H. F. Bergman made the first test crosses. Selections from these crosses resulted in three cultivars, 'Beckwith', 'Stevens', and 'Wilcox', that were released by the USDA in 1950. Three additional cultivars, 'Franklin', 'Bergman', and 'Pilgrim', were released in 1961.

There are a few others, but compared to apples or grapes, virtually no breeding has taken place. Today, Eric Stone at the Blueberry and Cranberry Experiment Station in Chatsworth, New Jersey, is the only person breeding cranberries. He is trying to create a cranberry vine with a higher yield of earlier, sweeter berries. It's a slow process: three to four years to examine the progeny of a single cross, ten to fifteen years before a named cultivar can be released. At present Stone is hybridizing existing stocks, and he speculates that the sugar content might be increased by crossing with *Vaccinium vitis-idaea*, the cowberry. He hopes to find money to explore for new breeding material.

Stone is a seasoned plant breeder, but he has been on the project only since 1978. Before that there seems to have been a general hiatus in interest. Even now Stone only works half-time—the other half of his time is spent breeding blueberries.

Growers complain that the available propagating stock they receive is too variable to be predictable; commercial processors complain that the berries aren't the right color; home cooks complain about how much sugar they have to add. You would expect to find a breeding program aimed at these complaints. More berries, redder berries, sweeter berries, berries that are easier to process, or berries that keep longer. These are more likely to come out of a breeding program than anywhere else. And yet there is only one man in the entire United States who is breeding cranberries. Is it not an inequitable and shortsighted distribution of resources to put so much effort into product development and advertising and so little into genetic improvement of the vine itself?

A major breeding campaign will require the sustained commitment of dollars and human energy for decades, not years. There will be no immediate benefits, and the slow return on the investment will be seen by many as a major obstacle. But the berries that come over this barrier would be the best yet.

18

MYCOLOGICAL

I t is generally understood that the oral ingestion of sacred mushrooms will induce colored visions, auditory hallucinations, and unearthly flights of fancy. What is less generally appreciated is that reading about mushrooms can sometimes induce similar effects.

The case concerns a 31-year-old, married, Caucasian male who, in the course of several weeks, subsisted entirely on an intellectual diet of books, pamphlets, and journal articles about mushrooms. Toxic exposure is presumed to have occurred through the eyes, although some dermal absorption through the hands cannot be ruled out. The species of mushrooms involved were principally edible ones, such as *Agaricus bisporus*, which are not known to contain any mycotoxins, and the patient reported no previous sensitivity to this or other subject matter. The following is the patient's own account of his symptoms.

I was reading in the library after lunch in a green leather armchair pulled up under the window where I could get some sun, when suddenly it was dark and I was surrounded by huge white mushrooms. They looked like mushrooms, but in spite of the gloom, I could just see that they weren't real mushrooms, but people wearing mushroom-shaped hats like the ones chefs wear. They were seated all around me quietly listening to an ant talk. The ant, a large brown one, was standing dead center on the ball head of a microphone attached to a podium, and its voice was coming over loud and clear, a cricketlike sound, each syllable rasped out but with the words perfectly understandable.

"Fellow mushroom growers," the ant said, "it is time for better relations between ants and humans. I don't need to describe what we have had to endure—the attacks on our nests, the daily humiliations of being stepped on. Why do you treat us this way? Do you think you have a monopoly in mycoculture? You are not the only mushroom growers, and you have no right to feel superior, for we ants have far more experience cultivating fungi than you humans. It was only yesterday that you stopped stoning mastodons for your meals.

"I have come here today to explain how we grow fungus and to pass on some advice about fungus culture in general. I hope that in response you will treat us more humanely. We have been observing your precocious attempts at mushroom culture, and although we are sometimes amused by your blundering, we are touched by how antlike much of your behavior is. A number of my colleagues objected to my coming here today, pointing out how much suffering you had caused us, but I reminded them of an old proverb we have that says 'Fungus eaters are sisters.'"

I heard one of the mushrooms behind me ask, "Is this for real?" "I think so," I whispered without turning around. "I remember reading about these ants somewhere."

"We belong to the great tribe Attini," the ant continued, "an association of nearly two hundred species divided into twelve genera. Our headquarters are in the American tropics, but we have offices as far north as the New Jersey Pine Barrens and as far south as the cold deserts of Central Argentina. My own colony, *Atta sexdens* Brazil 71-30-9006, was founded nearly seven years ago. Before leaving her birthnest, Her Royal Hugeness the Queen filled her infrabuccal pouch with fungal mycelium. The nuptial flight that followed was risky and romantic. It ended when, wingless and inseminated for life, she excavated a chamber for herself in the soil. Here she spat out the wad of fungal mycelia she was carrying and carefully began feeding the fungus with her Royal Feces: every hour she plucked a bit of fungus from the developing fungus garden, bent her abdomen between her legs, annointed the bit with amber fecal fluid, and replaced it in the garden. At the same time, Her Royal Hugeness was laying her first eggs, and when these hatched she had to feed them as well, since there were no nurses. For my infant sisters, she prepared omelets made from some of her own eggs. Such Royal Munificence! And all the time she was eating nothing herself, merely metabolizing her own fat and the wing muscles she no longer needed. When her firstborn emerged as adult workers, they became nurses and foragers and gardeners, and Her Hugeness could devote herself to egg laying. But this is history."

I looked around me and there were now more mushrooms, clusters of them sitting in the shadows. Perhaps they had been there all along and my eyes had only just become adapted to the dark. On the podium the ant was cleaning her antennae. She arranged her legs and continued.

"Our nest is now more than six meters wide. It has nearly two thousand chambers and two hundred fifty fungus gardens." A slide came on, a blueprint of the colony showing all the chambers, the galleries that connected them, and the locations of the outside entrances. There were red arrows rising from the middle of the nest and blue ones that led down into the galleries at the edges. "You will note," the ant explained, "that our nest is designed for passive ventilation. The heat that is generated by the fungus gardens in the center rises, drawing cool air down into the nest at the periphery. This is an entirely automatic system of ventilation that has no moving parts and powers itself." A number of mushrooms nodded their approval.

"Our fungus chambers are up to half a meter wide and are filled with a spongy mixture of mycelia and substrate. The garden, however, does not touch the soil walls of the chamber. To keep out soil-borne pests, the garden is suspended from clean rocks and roots.

"For a substrate we use fresh leaves, stems, and flowers, and this is no doubt why we are so maligned by humans. When we cut the leaves of a forest tree, no one notices, but when we gather the petals from a rosebush, we're called robbers and destroyers. Laws are even passed that declare us a plague. I acknowledge that it is alarming to have us remove leaves from a plant, especially if it happens to be cultivated coffee or citrus or cacao, but how many of you have noticed that we seldom remove all the leaves from a tree. We may be cutting leaves from a particular tree today, but tomorrow we will be cutting somewhere else. Since the founding of our own colony, we have harvested more than six thousand kilograms of leaves, but our nest is still surrounded by healthy vegetation.

"To collect these leaves my larger sisters travel out from the nest along a well-trimmed highway to the site of the day's cutting. If the trail runs across a lawn, the grass has all been clipped away until there is a smooth dirt path. Often the route leads up into the canopy along a liana or aerial root. When she has reached her destination, my sister stands on the edge of a leaf and begins to cut out a section of it with her mandibles, using her body as a radius to determine the size of the cut. When it has been sliced free, she hoists the piece over her head and joins the long procession of ants carrying pieces of leaves back to the nest. Some of you humans fancy that she is using the leaf to shield herself from the sun and so you call us parasol ants. Leaf cutters we may be, but parasol ants we are not. Sometimes one of my tiniest sisters rides on the leaf as it is being carried. Although she is extra weight, she can drive away any parasitic flies that may attack."

The darkness and the humidity were getting a bit much, and I was beginning to feel that something was crawling on me. It had also begun to rain. I slid over and tried to get under the edge of one of the mushrooms, but these commercial mushrooms don't have much of an edge.

The ant had moved underneath the microphone head to avoid the drip but continued speaking. Her sentences were punctuated by raindrops.

"The fresh plant matter that my sisters bring back to the nest is too large to add to the fungus-gardens directly, so it is first cut into smaller fragments, one to two millimeters across. (Drip) These are chewed around the edges to make them pulpy, fertilized with our own feces, and inserted in the fungus garden. (Drip) We transplant tufts of mycelium onto the surface of each new fragment, and within twenty-four hours the mycelium grows enough to cover the new substrate. The tending of the fungus garden is done entirely by my smallest sisters, who can move most easily through the intricate convolutions of the fungus garden. (Drip, drip) It amuses us to see your insistence that humans should perform any task regardless of how big or little you are. In our society the job you have depends entirely on your size. My largest sisters are soldiers, the next largest are foragers and excavators, sisters that are smaller yet have a variety of jobs in the nest, and the smallest of us are nurses and gardeners. It's the way to live.

"By now you are all aware that there are several differences between the way we grow our fungus and the way you grow *Agaricus bisporus*. In a number of ways our methods are better than yours."

When she said this, I realized that I was wearing a sticky tag on my lapel that said "Press" and that I was supposed to be reporting this conference. I fumbled in my pockets for something to write on. All I could find was some Kleenex, and it was damp.

"First of all we don't have to compost our substrate before we use it. You humans prefer to use horse manure, which you get from racetracks or riding stables, but you must pile it in long rows, 8 to 10 feet wide and as deep, and then repile it at least four more times, before the manure has decayed enough for your fungus to grow on it. That's a lot of weight to move over and over. We have read of your new 'liquid compost,' a mixture of water, beet molasses, cottonseed meal, urea, other chemicals, and a culture of microorganisms, which is poured over straw or corncobs. This you can mix and use immediately for growing mushrooms instead of waiting three weeks. It is an advance, but of course we have been doing it all along, except the liquid we add to the fresh leaves, stems, and flowers is our own feces, which we don't have to prepare separately.

"Furthermore, you humans insist on pasteurizing your compost by heating it to 57 degrees Celsius (135 degrees Fahrenheit, for those of you who have not yet adopted our temperature system). You have to do this to kill off a host of unwanted fungi that might be present. You are more familiar with the list than I; the ink caps, olive green mold, white plaster mold, soft mildew, lipstick mold, black whisker mold, and mat disease. You even have something you call calves' brains.

"We can't, of course, pasteurize our gardens. Such temperatures, even if we could generate them, would be hazardous to our own health. By keeping ourselves very clean, and by carrying leaves back to the nest instead of dragging them, however, we manage to cut down on the number of fungal spores we introduce. Keeping the garden away from the walls of the chamber also helps. Of greatest importance, however, is a mixture of chemicals we add to the substrate in our fungus gardens. These chemicals which we manufacture ourselves promote the growth of our fungus and inhibit the growth of others. I would tell you more about our special formula, but surely you all appreciate the importance of a few trade secrets.

"You humans buy the spawn with which you inoculate your pasteurized compost. This spawn, which is mycelia grown on sterile manure, rye grain, or tobacco stems, is broadcast over the compost and allowed to grow for three weeks, whereupon you 'case' the bed by covering it with a few centimeters of soil or peat moss. We ants don't have to go to someone else for our spawn, we simply take mycelium from an adjacent garden.

"Two weeks after you have cased the beds the first mushrooms appear. They continue to develop in flushes every seven to ten days for two to three months. Before the mushrooms are fully matured you pluck them, although in the process you destroy many young mushrooms by disrupting the mycelia.

"Here," said the ant, tapping three of her feet on the surface of the microphone for emphasis, "is an important difference between humans and ants. You eat the mushroom and we eat the mycelium. The fungus we grow forms globular swellings at the tips of the tubular filaments that make up the mycelia. These swellings you call 'gongylidia' or, more fancifully, 'heads of kohlrabi.' To us they are simply food. Plucked and eaten directly with no further preparation, they are our sole source of nutrition, a single food providing our minimum daily requirement of everything. We couldn't eat mushrooms even if we chose to, for the fungus we grow doesn't form mushrooms in our fungus gardens.

"You humans, however, have a choice between mushrooms and mycelia, between the cherry and the cherry tree, so to speak. By and large you choose the cherry. The fungi you eat, whether they are champignons, wood ears, shiitake, or morels, are all mushrooms. Not only do you restrict yourselves to the fruiting bodies of fungi, but you restrict yourselves to using them only for their flavor. The meager couple of pounds of mushrooms you eat each year appear as appetizers or as accents for soups and salads.

"You are not taking advantage of the protein in fungus," said the ant, stamping her feet again. "Each of you requires 65 grams of protein each day. That amounts to 52.2 pounds a year. By the end of the century you will be looking for 300 billion pounds of protein to feed the world's human population. Where will you get the protein? Ultimately it will come from green plants, since they alone are capable of total protein synthesis. The protein in most human crop plants, however, is in very dilute form. How many of you could eat the 20 pounds of sugarcane or the 13 pounds of manioc each day needed to get enough protein? This same plant matter, however, is an abundant source of carbohydrates, and fungi need only carbohydrates and an inorganic source of nitrogen to synthesize proteins. *Agaricus bisporus* can yield 60 pounds of mycelia from no more than 100 pounds of sugar. And that mycelia has a dried weight protein content of 49 percent.

"Consider the advantages of cultivating fungi in concert with plants. An acre of sugarcane when fed to fungi will ultimately result in three tons of protein. Compare this to the mere 800 pounds of protein you currently harvest from an acre of soybeans.

"An acre of corn will yield only 72 pounds of protein if

you feed it to cows. However, if you remove the protein the corn contains and feed the remaining starch to fungi, the yield becomes 540 pounds.

"You must stop thinking of fungi as garnishes that you add to your food to dress it up, and begin thinking of them as a main course. My sisters and I have been living on nothing else for generations. You could cultivate the fungi on many of the waste materials you now have: beet molasses, citrus-press water, corn-steep liquor, coffee-processing waste.

"I have just read of your experiments with *Fusarium graminareum* grown on an artificial medium of glucose syrup and ammonia. The nylon of the food trade you call the 45-percent-protein product that results. You have modified the texture of the mycelium so that it resembles meat fiber, and you have created imitation fish, chicken, ham, and veal with it. This is progress, but you are still worrying too much about how the fungus tastes, whether the public will accept the new food. Every year, the need for protein increases, and fungi can meet the need. How they taste will be less and less important."

Somewhere in the distance a telephone began to ring, and I heard footsteps approaching. The room was becoming lighter, and as it did, both the mushrooms and the ant began to disappear. The podium had nearly faded away, but I caught the ant's last words. "Fungus farms," she said, "so thoroughly myco-logical."

19

INHOUSE
OUTHOUSE

At our house the outhouse is the center of attention. Adults ask for tours; children get lessons. Talk of waste disposal has become a supper-table standard, right alongside the boiled rice. But after a second helping of carbon-nitrogen ratios and pathogenic bacteria, it is hard to remember that we only wanted a second toilet.

Elisabeth, the family historian, has traced our current preoccupation with privies back some sixty years to the time when an elderly couple sold the house fully furnished but asked the new owner if they might reserve one thing. Explaining that by now "these are so accustomed to our bottoms," they carried away the privy seats. In most country houses the kitchen is the focal point. In ours it seems to be the toilet. Or as Elisabeth says, the privy spirit is one of our lares and penates.

We needed another toilet. Our aging septic system, however, didn't look like it needed another toilet, even if we had been able to surmount the peculiar architecture of our house and make the connection. There ensued a knight's tour of novel waste-treatment systems, a survey that ended with an inhouse outhouse.

We already had one outhouse, a true backhouse, under an ancient red maple tree. But it had provided hospitality to porcupines and dry rot for decades, and one glance was enough to bring back all one's negative feelings about out-houses. The missing window, the door with only one rusty hinge, the threads of fungus reaching up from the decayed sill—these summoned memories of icy seats, mosquitoes and spiders, fears of bats, and the gaping black hole down which a camp counselor repeatedly threatened to deposit my pillow.

We knew that outhouses didn't have to be that way. We'd seen ones as clean, and white, and crisp as a nine-teenth-century hospital ward. We remembered venerable three-holers—two sizes for adults, a smaller one for children —whose whitewashed interiors without partitions invited conversation among occupants of the same sex. We had seen privies with slate roofs, with red geraniums in window boxes, with a magazine rack for the *New Yorker*. We even knew someone whose privy seat was solar heated. Instead of keeping the seat indoors behind the wood stove during the winter, he glassed in the south side of his privy and painted the throne black.

What attracted us most, however, were outhouse fun-damentals. With no plumbing there would be nothing to leak, or freeze, or clog. We wouldn't be wasting our pre-cious well water or contaminating someone else's lake. Truly, the muck would stop here. To be sure of this we were prepared to use a watertight receptacle. We were also planning ample venting and a modern decor. At this point someone suggested that having rendered our outhouse safe, odorless, and beautiful, we might as well have it indoors. Indoors it came, in the form of a Clivus Multrum.

The Clivus Multrum is to bathrooms what the Cuisinart is to kitchens—they are both rather pricey European food processors. Clivus Multrum is Swedish for "inclining compost room," and room size it is. Down in the cellar, and positioned so that it is beneath both bathroom and kitchen, a glossy, white fiberglass polyhedron—6 feet tall, 9 feet long, and 4 feet wide—reclines at a 30 degree angle. Two small doorways, or access ports, lead to the tank's pink interior, where a couple of tons of peat moss, human waste, and garbage quietly rot away. A series of baffles and air ducts assures that the decomposition stays aerobic. From the top of the tank, a galvanized metal duct 6 inches in diameter extends above the roof, pulling air through the tank and carrying off carbon dioxide and water vapor.

Except for a small electric fan in the vent pipe, the Clivus has no moving parts. Two 12-inch diameter chutes, one leading from the toilet to the tank and the other from the kitchen, deliver their material by gravity. Once inside the tank, these mix and molder, the residue sliding toward the exit at glacial speed.

The Clivus Multrum is a composting toilet, but it does not produce much compost—none at all for a couple of years and even in full operation only about 1½ cubic feet per person per year. The remainder goes up the vent in metabolic smoke. Repeated tests of the end product have shown the bacterial composition to be similar to soil. The carbon-nitrogen ratio compares favorably with that found in municipal and garden composts, although it contains substantially more nutrients. Unlike commercially processed sewage sludge, which may have been contaminated by industry, Clivus compost is relatively free of toxic metals.

The biggest problem with the Clivus Multrum is the difficulty of installing it in an existing building. Our Clivus was delivered—all 700 pounds of it—packed on a wooden pallet. Fortunately, the tank comes in two halves, like a giant bivalve, or it would never have made it through the door. With it came a 40-page *Planning Installation and Operation Manual for Residential Applications* that proclaimed "anyone with basic carpentry skills can install a Clivus Multrum" in "approximately 30 hours." We got the cradle built, the baffles installed, added the 20 cubic yards of peat moss and 2 inches of garden soil as an inoculum, and got ready to glue the two halves of the tank together. Because we felt we were well into our 30-hour allotment, and because the instructions with the adhesive said we had 20 minutes, we timed this step. We had to spread two tubes of adhesive and tighten twenty-eight sets of quarter-inch bolts and washers. There were five of us, each with our own wrenches, and it took 19 minutes 35 seconds.

The completed system is as easy to operate, however, as it is tricky to install. You have to remember to leave the toilet lid down, but there's no need to flush. Unlike spoons that have been through the disposal, silverware accidentally dumped with the garbage can be retrieved unscathed. Most of us have never been in the habit of putting glass, paint, or plastic down the toilet so it's easy to keep them out of the Clivus. The only major caution is required of those who smoke. Drop a lit cigarette into a Clivus and you risk igniting the contents. Firemen aren't likely to forget being called to extinguish an inhouse outhouse.

We had apprehensions about the Clivus Multrum, having heard tales of excess liquid in the compost and plagues of flies. One installation we visited before buying our own was yielding extra liquid (compost-water, *not* urine), but the owners solved the problem by filling empty wine bottles with the amber fluid and giving them away to visitors as safe, nutritious houseplant food. We find it simpler just to regulate the amount of liquid that enters the tank. Flies we have. Swarms of tiny, fruit fly-sized ones. But they stay in the tank, unable to compete with the downdraft when the toilet or garbage chute lids are opened. We could use a pesticide, but since the flies and their larvae are hastening decomposition, it would seem to defeat our purpose.

What has taken getting used to is not the tons of decaying waste in the cellar, but the number of people who want to see it as soon as they come in the front door. When guests are expected we no longer rush to make our beds. Instead we go downstairs, open up the access port, and neaten up the compost. It's not any worse than making a bed; even with your head and shoulders in the tank there is no odor other than that of fresh soil. What is harder to take is raising the toilet lid and hearing voices, a tour being conducted below. There's no stopping people. They want to see it, use it, talk about it. Although it's exhilarating to be a sewage-treatment pioneer, it requires some adjustment to go public with one's privy.

20

---·•·---

THE
UNGRACIOUS
HOST

O ne of the advantages, or side effects, of having children is that we become experts on subjects we might
otherwise have missed—from new wave music to horseman-
ship. While not the usual ingredients of adult education,
these lessons are about as avoidable as dirty socks. Simply
expect to learn about the maternity of guinea pigs or long
division in base seven. These were, remember, the sorts of
things we taught our parents. This said, I would rather not
have had to learn about head lice.

The first of these insects—tiny, wingless, and off-white
—was brought to my attention on the tip of a No. 2 pencil,
a pencil our 10-year-old son had just used to scratch his
head with. None of us remember what became of that
louse, for it was only the first of many. Although we have

had insect guests before—fireflies, caterpillars, and such—they soon died, escaped, or were let go. The head lice have been much more persistent guests. We are rid of them for now, but no one in the family is confident that they are gone for good.

We have not been gracious hosts. In fact, we seldom miss a chance to complain. "We have head lice," I tell other parents. "Head lights? How nice," they usually respond, trying to steer away from the subject. Head lice are not something people complain about, at least not in polite company, and yet there is currently an epidemic of them. After twenty or thirty years of relative absence following World War II, these irritating parasites are back in force.

At the Centers for Disease Control in Atlanta, they know how many people in the country came down with mumps or leprosy last week, but they do not know how many new cases of lice were discovered. This is because pediculosis—medicalese for being lousy—does not have to be reported to public health authorities.

There is, nevertheless, plenty of evidence that homework is not the only thing making children scratch their heads. The CDC investigated schools in New York, Georgia, and Florida in 1973 and 1974, checking the heads of 6,379 students from kindergarten through the eighth grade. The good news is that head lice are not a problem for blacks: only 0.3 percent of the black students had lice. The bad news is that of the nonblack students, 7 percent of the boys and 10 percent of the girls were lousy. Because the studies were carried out in schools that recognized they had a louse problem, it is risky to generalize from these statistics. In any given school the percentages may be lower, but they may also be higher. Furthermore, the problem is not limited to the United States. From Canada and Chile, from England, France, Italy, East Germany, the Soviet Union, even Australia, come reports of head lice infesting as many as 50 percent or more of the children in some schools.

Under the circumstances, it seems silly not to talk about having lice. People have not always been so inhibited. The residents of Hurdenburg, Sweden, used to choose their mayor by having eligible candidates sit around a table with their beards touching the tabletop. A louse was then dropped into the center and allowed to choose the winner.

Head lice belong to an order of insects known as sucking lice. The 250 species in the order all possess a claw on the end of each leg that folds against a thumblike projection, enabling the louse to grip tightly onto the hairs of its mammalian host. Sucking lice feed on the blood of many different mammals, but individual species are limited in their tastes. The lice that feed on walruses do not feed on carpenters.

Human beings play host to three sorts of lice. One of these, the crab louse (*Pthirus pubis*), is notorious as a sexual hazard. The broadly oval gray creatures with their slightly reddish legs are most frequently transmitted during intercourse, hence their French name *papillons d'amour*. It must be added that, contrary to popular belief, one *can* get crabs from toilet seats, although the rest-room graffito "Please to stand upon the seat, the crabs in here can jump six feet" is a gross exaggeration. Unlike fleas, lice cannot jump. Simply raising the toilet seat will cause them to fall off. Although they usually hang out in the pubic hair, crab lice can sometimes be found on coarse hair farther up the body—in armpits, beards, mustaches, eyelashes, and eye-brows. They can also occur in the hair of the head, but they do not survive there. In order to mate, male and female must grasp adjacent hairs and face each other, and the hairs of the scalp are simply too close together, it is thought, for these amatory acrobatics.

Crab lice are not our family's problem, fortunately. There is no mistaking them for head lice. Head lice are larger, and elongate rather than broad. The females are 2 to 3 millimeters long, a little larger and fatter than the males. Head lice can be confused with body lice, though, because they are very similar in appearance. Indeed, en-tomologists once assigned them both to the same species, *Pediculus humanus.*

Head and body lice may look the same, but they be-have very differently. Body lice are seldom if ever found on the head. They live in clothing when not actually feed-ing, and they cement their eggs on fibers of cloth. A change of clothes and a bath are enough to get rid of these "seam squirrels." They persist only among people who habitually live in their clothes—vagrants, soldiers at war. More serious than the itching that body lice cause are the diseases they transmit, especially epidemic (or louse-borne) typhus, which the bacteriologist Hans Zinsser claimed killed more people than any other disease. Between 1917 and 1923, some three million people in European Russia alone died of it.

Head lice, however, do not spread disease, and al-though they are capable of hybridizing with body lice they rarely do so, even if both kinds are living on the same person. For these and other reasons, the head louse has recently been assigned to a separate species, *Pediculus capitis*, to distinguish it from *Pediculus corporis*, the body louse. Whereas the body louse forsook body hair with the advent of clothing, the head louse has become superbly adapted to life in the hairy savannas of the scalp. It begins life as an egg cemented to the base of a hair. These yellowish white eggs, or nits, are surprisingly large—nearly a millimeter long. After incubating for seven to ten days, the young louse within pierces the egg with its proboscis, then swallows air and ejects it from its anus, thus forcing itself out of the shell by compressed air. (The empty nit remains attached to the hair shaft.) The newly emerged louse begins feeding at once. Ten days and three molts later, it is an adult, its body color having changed somewhat to match the color of the hair in which it lives.

Adult head lice live for about a month, during which time the female can lay fifty to a hundred eggs. Nits are usually the most conspicuous sign of head lice, because, for reasons no one knows, there are seldom more than ten to fifteen adults on a human head. Itchiness can also be a sign, although the first time a louse bites there is only a slight sting. It takes repeated bites before an allergic reaction occurs, with redness and itching. Sensitivity gives way eventually to immunity, but heavy infestations of head lice can cause secondary infections. In nineteenth-century Poland the fashion for tight fur caps and the belief that a lousy scalp was healthy led to a widespread outbreak of *plica polonica*, a mass of moist hair and lice on a filthy, inflamed scalp.

Such an image is disgusting enough, but combined with confusion about which louse is which, it is no wonder that parents react with alarm when they hear that a child has head lice—usually when he is sent home from school with a mimeographed note requesting that he not return until his hair is free of nits. Parents often respond with unfair accusations against the child and threats to shave his head. Even more devastating can be the taunts of classmates chanting "Cootie! Cootie!" at recess.

Perhaps the greatest myth about head lice is that they are a sign of uncleanliness. This may be true of body lice, but how often you shampoo your hair has nothing to do with whether or not you have head lice. Neither, for that matter, does the length of your hair or how often you comb it. Some parents like to point out that head lice and the Beatles became part of the American scene at about the same time. But so far, no one has been able to demonstrate a link between long locks and lice.

Explanations, all of them unsatisfactory, for why blacks in the United States and Europe rarely get head lice range from the shape of the hairs to the use of hair oil. Gender has something to do with the distribution of head lice. Girls, for unknown reasons, have a slightly greater risk of infestation than boys.

The most important determinant for lousiness may well be social distance. Young children are more susceptible than older ones, who in turn are more susceptible than adults. It is tempting to attribute the shortage of lousy adults to a biochemical immunity, especially when all your children have head lice and you do not. A more likely explanation is that with increasing years children maintain greater social distance and hence are less likely to touch heads. Among older children, social distance can be simply defined as "No, you can't borrow my comb."

Combs, brushes, scarves, hair ribbons, hats, batting

helmets, earphones, and towels can all pass head lice from scalp to scalp. Sharing a coat hook or a locker also improves chances of picking up lice. Actual head-to-head contact, of course, is a louse's dream.

Personally, we have done a lot to keep the lice at bay, but sooner or later, we expect to have them in the family again. We won't panic, and we won't try to fumigate the house. Once they are away from a head, adult lice can survive for only forty-eight to fifty-five hours at room temperature, and less than 10 percent of the eggs stuck to loose hairs will hatch after a week. Nits and lice are both killed by water that is hotter than 125 degrees Fahrenheit, so we will simply run clothing and bedding through the washing machine. Only garments that have been used within the last two days need be treated. Blankets and things that cannot be machine-washed will be sealed up in a plastic garbage bag and quarantined for ten days until any lice are dead.

As for the heads themselves, the best treatment is a medicated shampoo for lice. The most commonly used prescription drug is Kwell, which contains the insecticide lindane. We prefer to use one of the equally effective pyrethrin-based shampoos—A-200 Pyrinate, Rid, or Triple-X —because they are available over the counter and their active ingredients are less hazardous to human beings. As with all insecticides, directions must be followed explicitly.

These shampoos do not kill the nits, and a second application seven to ten days later is a good idea. Some schools will not have the children back if they have nits in their hair, dead or alive. If you ever wondered where the term nit-picking comes from, you learn. Actually only the nits close to the skin are cause for worry. Hair grows about 0.5 millimeters a day, so any nit more than a quarter of an inch from the scalp has either hatched already or never will hatch. Like any hunter on safari, you must be sure of your prey, for there are nits that are not. Globules of hair spray, flecks of paint, dandruff, and knotted hairs can all look a bit like a nit. Use a magnifying glass to be sure.

Nits can be removed one at a time, but as with gathering cranberries or low-bush blueberries, it is easier to use a rake. Special metal fine-tooth combs—Derbac and Medicomb are two models—have teeth spaced only 0.1 of a millimeter apart. They strip away the eggs neatly, but to avoid pulling out hair you should wet the head beforehand. Done properly, combing out is actually an enjoyable experience—at least for the recipient—the sort of grooming that other primates delight in.

All of this skirts the basic issue. Where does the blame lie for the world's oversupply of head lice, and what can we do about it? Some people blame the increasing resistance to insecticides, pointing out that some head lice have evolved an immunity to lindane. Resistance may well become a major explanation for an epidemic in the future, but I blame this one on widespread ignorance.

For a generation, we did not have to think about head lice, time enough to forget what they even looked like. Cootie catchers were paper traps used to pluck imaginary germs off other kids. Pinworms and polio were the things our parents talked about, not head lice.

At any time all that is needed for head lice to stage a comeback are parents who are too busy to notice a child scratching his head, pediatricians who are too rushed to check during checkups. A single child can infest an entire class. Even treating all the students in a school is not enough. Brothers and sisters at home are almost certain to have head lice as well. Unless everyone checks everyone else for them, they will be passed back and forth endlessly.

Head lice are going to remain abundant until all of us are once again familiar with the creatures. Until we swallow our disgust and begin to check routinely for nits. Until we start discussing head lice with one another. We might as well accept head lice as a necessary lesson that comes with parenthood. At least no one says we have to be gracious about them.

21

THE LAST
POINSETTIA
OF SUMMER

In a university town, chilly mornings and crimson leaves mark both a change of season and residence. Like hermit crabs moving from one empty shell to another, students and professors hurry to change domiciles, competing for the best residences and feeling exposed and vulnerable as long as everything they own is in the back of a station wagon. At this time of year even those who have become expert at maneuvering 36-inch desks through 35-inch doorways long for a permanent address. A high-interest mortgage could be no more burdensome than a sofa going up three flights.

Reviewers like to say that writers are gifted at examining the world around them, noting the homely details, capturing the moment. Many are, but it seldom shows.

Most writers—and certainly all the ones who aren't independently wealthy—scratch out a living not because they
are gifted at examining the present but because they are
gifted at recalling the past or guessing the future. They
rarely get an opportunity to examine the present. Editors
don't allow it.

Readers, editors tell authors, want seasonal articles,
ones that coincide with current events. But when time is
allowed for copyediting, typesetting, proofreading, paste-up,
photography, and printing, the deadline for any seasonal
story falls far in advance of the season itself. Like an Aus-
tralian visiting New York, writers must live by two calendars.

So it is that I celebrate the ninth month of the year not
with a tale of the neighbors' travels and travails but with a
tale about Christmas. Out my window students are stuffing
pillows around an old lamp, but writing turns my vision
inward, where the view isn't as good. Squinting through the
haze of other memories, stretching to see over plans for the
iris bed, craning to look past a list of things I'm remembering to buy, I can just glimpse paper-white narcissus in a
blue-porcelain bowl, flat white boxes and torn tissue paper,
a whiff of oranges studded with cloves, mittens on a radiator. O, Father Christmas, won't you please give me clair-
voyance and a perfect recall.

I mustn't object. I have my muse beside me on the
desk, a poinsettia from last Christmas—still in bloom. The
actual flowers, tiny greenish yellow ones in a cuplike struc-
ture, are long gone, but the showy petallike leaves or bracts
are hanging on. I think they have lost some of their in-
tensity, but this might just be dust. I wish I could say that I
was responsible for my poinsettia's longevity, that I was
being rewarded for carefully keeping the plant away from

hot radiators and chilly windowpanes, that I was careful not to give the plants so much water that the leaves turned yellow and dropped or so little that they wilted, or that I had lavished the plant with fertilizer. But I haven't, and therein lies a tale.

The poinsettia (*Euphorbia pulcherrima*) is native to the southern Mexican states of Guerrero, Oaxaca, and Chiapas, where it is a gangly, woody, evergreen shrub 15 feet tall. The Aztecs called the poinsettia *cuetlaxachitl* and regarded the plant as a symbol of purity. Following the Christian invasion, it became a symbol of Christmas and was rechristened *flor de Pascua* or *flor de buena noche*.

Joel Roberts Poinsett (1779–1851), a native of Charleston, South Carolina, served as U.S. ambassador to Mexico from 1825 to 1829 and was responsible for introducing to this country the plant which now bears his name. Although no contemporary correspondence appears to have survived, it is thought that he sent seeds or plants back to Charleston in 1828. While he may have been interested in poinsettias as a depilatory, a cure for skin infections, a milk stimulant for nursing mothers, a windbreak in cornfields, a source of red dye, or one of the other indigenous uses of the plant, it seems more likely that it was the bright red flowers, appearing in midwinter, that drew his attention to this tropical shrub.

A Colonel Carr, husband of John Bartram's granddaughter Ann, is said to have visited Charleston and, seeing the poinsettias, arranged shortly thereafter for their first public showing at an exposition of the Philadelphia Horticultural Society in 1829. Robert Buist, a prominent Philadelphia seedsman, spotted them there and introduced them to the trade.

A century later, poinsettias had become as much of a Christmas tradition as mistletoe, but they were far from the perfect gift. First of all, they tended to grow too tall. Generations of horticulturists got their first greenhouse experience as youngsters bending back and tying down the tops of poinsettias in a crude effort to keep the plants within bounds. Second, the slightest stress caused blooming plants to shed their leaves. A fern in the center of each pot was used to hide the plant's bare limbs, for a bare bent stem, even with a full red crest, was about as popular in a parlor as a plucked chicken.

Things improved somewhat in 1923, when a Mrs. Enteman discovered a seedling poinsettia growing in Jersey City, New Jersey, that kept its leaves until Christmas. The progeny of this seedling, termed the 'Oak Leaf' poinsettia, became widely grown, and mutations or sports of 'Oak Leaf' accounted for most of the commercial poinsettias grown until the mid-1960s.

Lost leaves weren't the only liability of the early poinsettias. The bracts tended to be short-lived as well. Growers had to time their production precisely to be sure of a red Christmas. With flowers that often lasted only a couple of weeks, it was all too easy to miss the blessed day completely.

Poinsettias begin to develop flowers whenever there is a dark period of twelve hours or more each night. Under natural conditions this first occurs about October 5 in the poinsettia-producing parts of the Northern Hemisphere. Interrupting the night with a short spell of light will keep them from blooming indefinitely. So will streetlights, adjacent shopping malls, and passing cars. While some growers use night-lights to postpone blooming, those who want to guarantee that their poinsettias bloom, or want them to bloom precociously, encase their plants in black shade cloth from 5:00 P.M. to 8:00 A.M. every night, giving them fifteen hours of uninterrupted darkness.

By tinkering with night length, temperature, fertilizer, and the like, growers became adept at getting poinsettias to bloom seven to ten days before Christmas. But to say that the pots looked handsome when they were sold is not to say that they looked like much by New Year's. In the less-than-ideal environment of most homes, most poinsettias dropped everything.

Over the years, improved cultivars were selected, many by the firm of Paul Ecke Poinsettias of Encinitas, California, specialists in growing poinsettias since 1909. New cultivars were somewhat stockier and had a higher percentage of well-formed bracts that were wider, thicker, and redder. The bracts of tetraploid cultivars extended horizontally instead of drooping like diploid ones. There were poinsettias with white bracts and pink bracts, and poinsettias with incurved bracts that made the bloom look like a dahlia, but they all tended to be short-lived.

The best of the lot was 'Ecke White', a seedling that was first distributed in 1945. This and a sport, 'New Improved Ecke White' of 1958, were the only poinsettias that held their leaves and bracts both in the greenhouse and once they were sold. For a long time white poinsettias were thought to be the only ones capable of lasting, as though redness and pinkness were genetically linked to a short life.

There were occasional exceptions. A poinsettia flower here or there would hang on, outliving its peer group like some lonely centenarian. The owners of these diehards wrote letters to editors. In 1946 Mrs. Ora Kehn of Arvada, Colorado, had a red poinsettia last until May 1. Aeneas

Constantine of Harrisville, Michigan, went her one better with two poinsettias that persisted until June 9. This, however, was not the rule.

In the 1950s, several breeding programs to improve the poinsettia were begun. At Pennsylvania State University, the University of Maryland, and the USDA at Beltsville, Maryland, as well as at several commercial farms, breeders began hybridizing poinsettias in search of ones that would retain both leaves and bracts. 'Ecke White' was a frequent parent.

The first success was 'Paul Mikkelson', bred by Mikkelson's in Ashtabula, Ohio, and released in 1964. A cross between 'Ecke White' and one red seedling, this was the first poinsettia with exceptional keeping quality. From it sported a white, a pink, and a totally new color pattern, a bract with a pink midrib surrounded by white, a color combination now termed marbled. 'Paul Mikkelson' was soon followed by cultivars from other breeding programs, poinsettias with names like 'Eckespoint C-1 Red', 'Nebraska Red', 'Go Big Red', 'Rudolph', and 'Red Baron'. The final major improvement has been a series of basally branching poinsettias. 'Annette Hegg', introduced in 1968 by the Norwegian firm of Thormod Hegg and Sonn, was the first poinsettia to branch even without pinching, resulting in a single plant with as many as ten blooms.

As a result of all this attention, poinsettias have now joined Christmas lights as a harbinger of Thanksgiving. The one on the desk here beside me was in bloom at least a month before Christmas, a month it spent in a dark little shop without windows. By December 26 its leaves and bracts were all intact, but its market value had dropped badly and it was being given away. I carried it home wrapped in a couple of layers of newspaper and gave it to Elisabeth as a late present. She was happy to have it as a centerpiece for the table. After New Year's she was happy to have it on the sideboard. After Valentine's day she mumbled something about having had enough red and suggested I move it to the bookshelf. Actually, she suggested moving it to the rubbish. But how could anyone discard something still in mint condition? From Easter until Memorial Day, the poinsettia dropped a few bracts, becoming less symmetrical, but it was still flamboyant. I thought we should still keep watering it, Elisabeth thought not. By mid-July I resolved to keep the plant to myself.

By now, even I am getting tired of it. If I'd wanted a poinsettia with a lifetime guarantee, I could have bought a plastic one, one that I could have run through the dishwasher when it got dusty. I thought that having a poinsettia beside me would make it easier to be eloquent about December; it hasn't. Poinsettias ought to be a holiday event as precisely timed and short-termed as Santa's arrival. About that I can be enthusiastic. Our greatest enthusiasms, in fact, tend to be reserved for delights of short duration: maple-syrup making, strawberries, fireworks, childhood.

Change, not constancy, best serves the pencil, sharpening both memory and anticipation. Fortunately, life has a predilection for change, making it easy both to savor the good and withstand the bad, to enjoy ripe mulberries and endure gypsy moths. We no more need poinsettias year-round than we need head lice. Falling snow will give way to falling apple blossoms. And those fragile white petals, suffused in pink, settling down into the long meadow grass, will be something to remember.

22

HAMBURGERS AND HOUSEPLANTS

Marvel for a moment at the commonness of hamburgers and houseplants. Both the philodendron and the all-beef patty are now staples of American life. No one pulls the shades at night, not because modesty has been forgotten, but because shade pulling has become both impossible and unnecessary—so dense are the flowerpots on the windowsills, so thick are the leaves against the glass. Humidity is up, headroom is down. Trip over the potted palm beside the sofa and risk being throttled by verdant macrame on the way down. Plants threaten to take over all but the darkest corner of every room, and yet we go on accumulating new ones, an unusual maidenhair fern one week, a cute little peperomia the next.

When we aren't buying houseplants, we are buying

hamburgers. Millions of them. Blue-cheese burgers at business lunches, Big Macs with the kids. College students have an Elsie's Burger if they miss dinner, a triple cheeseburger at The Grill to get through the night. Once upon a time we ate tunafish sandwiches, peanut butter and jelly, cream cheese and olive. Now we eat hamburgers. We want them fast; we want them cheap. In return, we will tolerate jingles, billboards, and yellow arches.

We all know how common houseplants and hamburgers are. Few of us realize what they have in common. Houseplants are being treated as appliances. A fully furnished apartment comes with an air conditioner, a microwave oven, and a parlor palm. You can buy these all at K-Mart, and this gives the impression that, like other appliances, the indoor greenery originated in Chicago, Detroit, or West Bend. It did not. The Christmas cactus came from Brazil; the anthurium, from Colombia; the flaming sword, from French Guiana. Plant after plant is the descendant of some specimen collected by a plant hunter in tropical South America. *Aphelandra, Billbergia, Codonanthe, Dieffenbachia*—even a partial list would run through the alphabet and back.

Anyone who stops to think about the cultural requirements of our houseplants might deduce their tropical origin. Few would suspect it about hamburgers. On the menu there is always a picture of a Black Angus or Hereford steer, belly deep in western grass. Hamburgers are an American product all right, but not necessarily a North American one. The beef in the next hamburger you eat may well have come from Latin America.

In 1978, when the price of beef increased 35 percent in

five months, the U.S. government decided to increase the amount of imported beef. Imported beef is much cheaper than beef grown in the United States. The 1978 wholesale price of beef imported from Central America was $1.47 per kilogram, compared to $3.30 for grass-fed beef grown in the United States. Although the amount of imported beef came to less than 1 percent of the total beef eaten in this country, government economists calculated that the imports would cut five cents off the price of every hamburger.

The government economists did not mention what increasing our consumption of imported beef would do to houseplants. The herds of Brahman cattle whose beef is shipped to the United States to be made into hamburgers and other processed meats are being raised on the same ground our houseplants came from. From Mexico to Brazil, tropical rain forests are being cut down to make new pastures. In some instances, the forest is simply doused with herbicide and set afire when the foliage dries out. In others, axes, chain saws, and bulldozers do the job. In any case, seldom is any of the wood even saved, so great is the pressure to get grass started and cattle herds established. Approximately 20,000 square kilometers of tropical rain forest in Latin America is being destroyed every year. Put another way, it will take less than six years to clear an area the size of Pennsylvania. One-quarter of all the forests in Central America have been destroyed in the last twenty years. Even the great forests of the Amazon are imperiled by Brazil's determination to become the world's biggest exporter of beef.

Boxcar statistics fail to capture the drama of felling even a single forest giant. As the chain saw begins to cut into a supporting buttress, spewing a plume of bright red sawdust, the parrots, the toucans, the oropendolas, and the howler monkeys who have been feeding in the tree's crown flee noisily. As the vibrations and exhaust reach them, the bats hanging upside down in the tree's interior awake from their day's sleep. Higher up the trunk, stingless bees pour out of a wax tube that marks the entrance to their nest. Out on a limb, thousands of ants rush about in search of the intruder. In the crown, nearly a hundred feet from the ground, the *Anolis* lizards, several species of frogs, a tree boa, and a sloth all sense that something is amiss, but they are all too small or too slow to do anything about it.

With all the buttresses on one side cut away, the sawyer begins the backcut. In only a moment the huge tree begins to lean. The sawyer, doing what none of the tree's inhabitants can do, flees to safety. Lianas, some as thick as a man's leg and as sinewy, hang from the tree and link it to adjacent smaller ones. For a moment it seems as though they might keep it from falling. But the tree's crown has too many epiphytes growing in it, too much moss, too many ferns, orchids, and bromeliads. The very luxuriance of the tree's canopy will speed its death. Lianas drawn tight snap the lesser trunks. The great tree, joined by its neighbors, crashes to the ground. It does not even bounce. When a tornado hits a cathedral, it is a tragedy. When such a tree falls, no one mourns. Whether its inhabitants are killed by the impact, or by desiccation, or incinerated in the fires that will shortly sweep through is unimportant.

Who knows what new medicines are being consumed by the flames, what oils, resins, dyes, spices, and insecticides; what unique genetic material that might someday be used for breeding; what plants that might someday grace our homes? Five out of six tropical organisms have never been identified, but that is not important.

What is important is cows. Slow, stupid, introduced beasts who know nothing of the grandeur that once occupied the ground on which they stand. It takes four years for them to reach full size; then they are slaughtered and their carcasses are reduced to hamburgers.

In less than a decade, the soil is too poor to grow grass, heavy rains have washed out the nutrients, erosion has scarred the land. Even heavy applications of fertilizer will not restore it. Scrub growth on which the cattle will not feed takes over. This is no problem. The rancher simply moves on to another piece of primary rain forest and starts again.

What can we do? Obviously, we can cut down on the amount of beef we eat. During World War I, the hamburger was renamed the Liberty Burger. Let's rename it once more. Call it a "rain forest burger" and eat fewer of them.

While we are changing our eating habits, we can also support the preservation of tropical forests directly. There is an urgent need to set aside large tracts of forest, to guard them against disturbance, to buy time while we study them and educate ourselves.

The responsibility for this conservation ultimately rests with the Latin American governments themselves. Fortunately, many are realizing that cutting down forests to raise beef is a sort of reverse alchemy, turning gold into silver. A host of international agencies such as the World Wildlife Fund in Washington, D.C., now recognize that to save species, both plant and animal, from extinction, their habitats must be preserved. They are collecting private contributions, using the money to help Latin American governments buy land for preservation.

A leading example is Costa Rica, a country with an unusually stable democracy situated between Panama and Nicaragua. Since 1969, Costa Rica has set aside 7 percent of its total landmass in national parks. The United States, by comparison, has less than 1 percent in national parks. To be sure, Costa Rica has cut down its share of rain forest to raise cattle and exported its share of beef, but the country is also blessed with the leadership of singularly farsighted individuals, both private citizens and government officials, who recognize that the rain forests will someday be worth more than any cattle pasture.

Unfortunately, the benefits to Costa Rica are in the future. The costs are in the present. While foreign organizations contributed $163,000 in 1975 to help Costa Rica establish Corcovado Park, a 290-square-kilometer preserve in the last undisturbed section of lowland rain forest in Central America, the Costa Rican people contributed $2 million—approximately one dollar for every man, woman, and child. And these are not people who can afford to eat hamburgers every day.

There is something we can do to hasten the return on Costa Rica's investment. It is very simple. Many of us take midwinter vacations. Will it be to the beaches of some Caribbean island or to the rain forests of Costa Rica? Our homes are filled with plants of the forest, but how many of us have ever seen *Dieffenbachia* in bloom or frogs depositing their tadpoles in the tanks of bromeliads? There are no orchid bees to pollinate the ones on our windowsills. To see our houseplants in their native habitat is to vastly enlarge our understanding and enjoyment of them. Visitors cannot help but return the wealthier, at the same time having helped to convince the country that conservation pays.

For years, we have been unwittingly feeding on tropical rain forests, consuming them bite by bite. It is time we put our money where our mouths are.

23

CAPTAIN'S LOG

Grandfather's great-grandfather, Captain Eliakim Gardner, traded sealskins to the Cantonese. He was a Nantucket sea captain, master of the merchant vessel *Orozimbo* out of Baltimore. His voyages lasted a year and a half or more because ships in the China Trade anchored off Patagonia, the Falkland Islands, Tierra del Fuego, or Chile while the crews went ashore to hunt seals. Only when the holds were full of salted hides did the ships set out across the Pacific Ocean for the port of Canton. There the sealskins were exchanged for cargos of porcelain, tea, and the yellowish cotton cloth called nankeen, all of which could be profitably sold to wholesalers back in New York, Philadelphia, and Boston.

One of the nine sons of a Nantucket shoemaker,

Eliakim Gardner was born in 1771, and in 1793 he married Pamela Gardner, a distant cousin. Their first child, Timothy, was born five years later, and a second, Nathan, six years after that. Generously spaced offspring were an unavoidable side effect of long voyages. Too often, the absences became permanent. The walks on Nantucket rooftops—lookouts enclosed in white balustrades—were a constant reminder that many men never returned. Three of Eliakim's older brothers, Grindal, Isaac, and Abraham, were lost at sea. And in August of 1808, stricken with fever, Captain Eliakim Gardner died in Batavia in the Dutch East Indies.

In addition to his wife and two sons, he left behind a portrait of himself painted in Amsterdam in 1801. He is dressed in a double-breasted gray coat with a dark velvet collar, a black-and-white-striped waistcoat, and a ruffled shirt. His hair, which extends down to his collar in back, has been fashionably powdered, and combed to hide a balding forehead. The solemn face that stares out of the oval in the cracked and chipped square gold frame is only 30. But it is a captain's face, a face that has seen many ports and weathered many storms. It looks years older.

Of my thirty-two great-great-great-grandparents, Eliakim Gardner is the one I feel closest to. Not simply because I know his face, but because I think of him as a restless man. I imagine him overseeing the loading of barrels of fresh water in some foreign harbor, eager to be sailing for home. I imagine him pacing the wharf in Nantucket, eager to see waves breaking on coral reefs once again. I imagine these things because I like to think there is an ancestral predilection for what one of my elementary school teachers once referred to as my "total inability to sit still." She thought I would eventually settle down, but this seems as unlikely now as it was during milk-and-cookies. In even the best library, surrounded by shelf after shelf of scholarship, I find myself thinking of hewing wood. But after a week with an axe or a crowbar, I am ready for books, lectures, great debates—in short, a change of clothes. Thus I journey back and forth between city and country. A "combination of Cambridge and cow chips" is how one reviewer described a collection of my writings, but I claim the phrase as a personal epithet.

Looking back over the preceding chapters, I find a record of my voyages, a sort of captain's log, albeit a largely terrestrial one. The entries were inscribed one by one, each limited to the matter at hand, but reading through the completed volume is like opening up a cardboard box into which you have been dropping vacation postcards for years. It is surprising to find how many places you have been. I set out to write about the science of the familiar—what causes hay fever, how birds know it is spring, why potted poinsettias last forever. These are the sorts of homespun questions a backyard biologist gets asked. In composing answers, however, I find that I have crossed continents and centuries. I could not account for mulberry trees in vacant lots without calling on the seventeenth century and its dreams of American silk. I could not champion the chore of spring rock picking without describing a Japanese temple garden. Eliakim Gardner kept a log because he traveled; I have traveled because I write.

If the captain's face looked older than his years, it reflected his responsibility for his ship and her crew. My journeys have been less perilous, but they have left me feeling no less responsible. I worry about the world's well-being, and not just because I need foreign for-instances to shore up my explanations of familiar phenomena. If I were to put down my pencil for good, it would not free me from care. One cannot travel far these days without discovering how much that we consider familiar comes from somewhere else. Whether one is walking among the olive trees of Tuscany or passing a barge loaded with Brazil nuts in Amazonia, notions of self-sufficiency vanish. And if one acknowledges even these simple debts, it is hard to ignore what goes on outside one's own backyard. All news becomes local news. A lake polluted, a forest burned, a species gone extinct—these are no longer things that happened somewhere else to someone else.

Despite the predictions that we are in for heavy weather, despite the possibility that there will be no future generations, I remain an optimist. Yes, we are capable of contaminating our air and water with more far-reaching consequences than ever before. Yes, we have made terrible blunders in the past. But we have also rescued a few lakes, and we are learning to live with gypsy moths. Let these be inspiration as we set about to ensure that there will be tropical forests for our grandchildren. But the longer we wait, the harder it will be. This is no time for anyone to sit still.

FURTHER
READING

Firewood

Firewood Crops: Shrub and Tree Species for Energy Production.
Washington, D.C.: National Academy of Sciences, 1980.
Stanford, G. "Coppicing Your Home Woodlot." *The Next Whole Earth Catalog.* New York: Point/Random, 1980, p. 84.

Avocados

Cook, R. E. "Attractions of the Flesh." *Natural History* 91:1 (1982): 20–24.
Heuvelmans, B. *On the Track of Unknown Animals.* Cambridge, Mass.: MIT Press, 1965.
Janzen, D. H., and Martin, P. S. "Neotropical Anachronisms: The Fruits the Gomphotheres Ate." *Science* 215:4528 (1982): 19–27.
Kurten, B., and Anderson, E. *Pleistocene Mammals of North America.* New York: Columbia University Press, 1980.

White Bloomers

Neary, J. "The Search for a White Marigold." *Horticulture* 54:2 (1976): 20–28.

Waser, N. M., and Price, M. V. "Pollinator Choice and Stabilizing Selection for Flower Color in *Delphinium Nelsonii.*" *Evolution* 35:2 (1981): 376–390.

Northern Comfort

Addicott, F. T. *Abscission.* Berkeley: University of California Press, 1982.

Chabot, B. F., and Hicks, D. J. "The Ecology of Leaf Life Span." *Annual Review of Ecology and Systematics* 13 (1982): 229–259.

Guests at Work

Benson, T. *Building the Timber Frame House.* New York: Scribners, 1980.

Perrin, N. *Amateur Sugar Maker.* Hanover, N. H.: University Press of New England, 1972.

Spring Time

Cornell, J. *The First Stargazers: An Introduction to the Origins of Astronomy.* New York: Scribners, 1981.

Pengelley, E. T., and Asmundson, S. J. "Annual Biological Clocks." *Scientific American* 224:4 (1971): 72–79.

Pengelley, E. T., ed. *Circannual Clocks: Annual Biological Rhythms.* New York: Academic Press, 1974.

Prerau, D. S. "Changing Times: National Time Management Policy." *Technology Review* 79:5 (1977): 55–63.

Crowbars, Glaciers, and Zen Temples

Fukuda, K. *Japanese Stone Gardens*. Rutland, Vt.: Charles E. Tuttle, 1970.

Washburn, A. L. *Periglacial Processes and Environments*. New York: St. Martin's Press, 1973.

Gypsy Moths

Doane, C. C., and McManus, M. L., eds. *The Gypsy Moth: Research Toward Integrated Pest Management*. Forest Service, Science and Education Agency, Animal and Plant Health Inspection Service Technical Bulletin 1584. Washington, D.C.: USDA, 1981.

Forbush, E. H., and Fernald, C. H. *The Gypsy Moth*. Boston: Wright and Potter, 1896.

McManus, M. L.; Houston, D. R.; and Wallner, W. E. *The Homeowner and the Gypsy Moth: Guidelines for Control*. USDA Home and Garden Bulletin No. 227, 1979.

Mulberry Visions

Bailey, L. H. *Sketch of the Evolution of Our Native Fruits*. New York: Macmillan, 1898.

Smith, J. R. *Tree Crops: A Permanent Agriculture*. New York: Devin-Adair, 1950.

Bee Bites

Pistorius, A. "Arthritis Relief: A Bee Sting Away?" *Country Journal* 5:5 (1978): 38–41.

Rubenstein, H. S. "Allergists Who Alarm the Public." *JAMA* 243:8 (1980): 793–794.

————. "Bee-Sting Diseases: Who Is at Risk? What Is the Treatment?" *The Lancet* 1:8270 (1982): 496–499.

Snodgrass, R. E. *Anatomy of the Honey Bee.* Ithaca, N.Y.: Comstock Publishing Associates, 1956.

A Drink You Can Swim In

Eutrophication: Causes, Consequences and Correctives. Washington, D.C.: National Academy of Sciences, 1969.

Lind, O. T. *Handbook of Common Methods in Limnology.* St. Louis: C. V. Mosby, 1979.

Wetzel, R. G. *Limnology.* Philadelphia: W. B. Saunders, 1975.

Trackside

Muhlenbach, V. "Contributions to the Synanthropic (Adventive) Flora of the Railroads in St. Louis, Missouri, USA." *Annals of the Missouri Botanical Garden* 66:1 (1979): 1–108.

Sophisticated Flypaper

Dethier, V. G. *Man's Plague: Insects and Agriculture.* Princeton, N.J.: Darwin Press, 1976.

Shorey, H. H., and McKelvey, J. J., Jr. *Chemical Control of Insect Behavior: Theory and Application.* New York: John Wiley and Sons, 1977.

Ill Winds

Salvaggio, J. E., ed. "Primer on Allergic and Immunological Diseases." *JAMA* 248:20 (1982): 2579–2772.

Samter, M. "Allergy and Clinical Immunology Fifty Years from

Now." *Journal of Allergy and Clinical Immunology* 64:5
(1979): 321–330.
Wodehouse, R. P. *Hayfever Plants*. Waltham, Mass.: Chronica
Botanica, 1945.

Mycological

Gray, W. *The Use of Fungi as Food and in Food Processing*
(Parts I and II). Cleveland: CRC Press, 1970, 1973.
Weber, N. A. *Gardening Ants, the Attines*. Philadelphia: Ameri-
can Philosophical Society, 1972.

Inhouse Outhouse

Farallones Institute. *The Integral Urban House: Self-Reliant
Living in the City*. San Francisco: Sierra Club Books, 1979.
Van Der Ryn, S. *Toilet Papers: Designs for Dry Toilets, Grey-
water Systems, and Recycling Human Wastes*. Santa Barbara,
Calif.: Capra Press, 1978.

The Ungracious Host

Andrews, M. *The Life That Lives on Man*. New York: Taplinger
Publishing Co., 1977.
Zinsser, H. *Rats, Lice, and History*. Boston: Little, Brown, 1935.

Hamburgers and Houseplants

Ayensu, E. S., ed. *Jungles*. New York: Crown, 1980.
Forsyth, A., and Miyata, K. *Tropical Nature*. New York: Scrib-
ners, 1984.
Myers, N. *The Sinking Ark: A New Look at the Problem of
Disappearing Species*. New York: Pergammon Press, 1979.

INDEX

Adams, Caswell, 83
Agaricus bisporus (mushroom), 165–74
ailanthus: firewood, 5; source of silk, 90
albino flowers, 16–25
alder, for firewood, 5
algal bloom, 110
Allard, H. A., 50–51
allergy: bee sting, 101–3; pollen, 133–42
aluminum sulfate, 114
anemophilous flowers, 136
Anolis (lizard), 199
anthocyanins, 18
antlers, development of, 52–53
ants, leafcutter, 166–74
Apanteles melanoscelus (wasp), 76
aphids, parthenogenetic, 52
Apis mellifera (honeybee), 96–103; pollen collected by, 140–42
apitherapy, 101
apple maggot flies, 127, 129–30
Aquilegia caerulea (columbine), 17

archaeoastronomy, 45–46
Archimedes, on levers, 57
Arrowsmith, Alan, 21–22
ash, white, 6, 68
aspen, coppice of, 6
Atta sexdens (leafcutter ants), 167–74
avocados, dispersal of, 9–15
axis of rotation, earth's, 45

Bacillus thuringiensis (bacteria), 70, 130
bacteria: in composting toilet, 177; in gypsy moth control, 70, 130; in lakes, 112
Bain, H. F., 163
balsam fir, 34–35, 68
basswood (*Tilia*), coppice of, 6
bats: in outhouses, 176; as pollinators, 136; tree dwelling, 199
beech, European: bud break of, 51; photosynthesis of, 29
Beecher, Henry Ward, 92
bees: orchid, 202; stingless, 199. *See also* honeybees
beetles: bark, 130; ground, 75;

Japanese, 128; vector of Dutch elm disease, 127
Benson, Ted, 38
Bergman, H. F., 163
biological control, 75–78, 131
biological oxygen demand, 109, 113
birds: accidental, 122; Boston ivy and, 84; gypsy moths and, 76–77; migration of, 48–50, 53; mulberries and, 87, 90; pollination by, 23–24, 136
blacklight traps, 126–27, 130, 132
bleeding heart (*Dicentra*), 16–17, 22
Blepharipa pratensis (tachinid fly), 76
blueberry: albino, 17; breeding, 164; origin of, 152
blue-eyed grass, albino, 17
blue-green algae, in lakes, 111
blue jays, gypsy moths and, 77
blue mustard (*Chorispora tenella*), 121
body lice (*Pediculis corporis*), 183
Bombyx mori (silk moth), 72, 87–90
Boston ivy (*Parthenocissus tricuspidata*), 79–85
bottled water, 104–5
boulders, definition of, 56
Brown, Royden, 141
Buist, Robert, 191
bumblebees, as pollinators, 23–24
burdock (*Arctium minus*), 121
Burpee, David, 19–20
butter-and-eggs (*Linaria vulgaris*), 121
by hook or by crook, 7

cardinal flower, albino, 17
caribou, antlers of, 52
carotenoids, 18
carp, 111, 113
castor bean (*Ricinus communis*), 119
Cathey, Marc, 20–21
cattle: beef, 197–98, 200–201; dung as fuel, 4; reforestation and, 5; seed dispersal by, 120

Ceriaco, Jose, 10, 12
chain saws, 2, 8, 198–99
Chandler, F. B., 162
Chasseneux, Bartholomaeus, 125
chestnut, coppice of, 6, 8
chickadees, gypsy moths and, 77
chickens, egg laying of, 50
chipmunks, gypsy moths and, 77
chokecherry, albino, 17
Christmas trees, 34–35
chrysanthemum, white, 21
circadian rhythms, 53
circannual rhythms, 53
Clemens, Samuel, 104
Clivus Multrum, 177–79
Cobb, Jonathan, 89
cobbles, definition of, 56
cockroaches, 123–24, 127–28, 131–32
Columella, Lucius Junius Moderatus, 126
compost, mushroom, 170–72
composting toilet, 175–79
conservation: candle, 47; firewood, 4–5; lake, 113–16; tropical forest, 200–202; wildflower, 17–18
copper sulfate, 113
coppices, 6–8
corn earworm, 131–32
county fairs, 144–51, 158–61
cowberry (*Vaccinium vitis-ideae*), 164
crab lice (*Pthirus pubis*), 182
cranberries, 152–64
creeping bellflower (*Campanula rapunculoides*), 119
crows: gypsy moths and, 77; migration of, 50
crowbars, 55, 57, 59, 61
cultural eutrophication, 112–13
Curtis, Will C., 17
Cypripedium reginae (showy lady's slipper), albino, 18

Dailey, Clarence, 146
Darlington, Thomas, 155
Darwin, Charles, 82
day-length, effects of, 44–54, 192–93

Daylight Savings Time, 47–48
day-neutral plants, 51
deciduous habit of plants, 27–29,
31–34
deer, antlers of, 52–53
deforestation, 4, 198–202
Delphinium nelsonii (larkspur),
23–24
Demoranville, Irving, 162
Dicentra spectabilis (bleeding
heart), 16–17, 22
Dill, J. P., 73–74
drawdown, of lakes, 115
ducks, testes of, 50, 53
dung, as fuel, 4

Ecke, Paul, 193
eight-spotted forester moth, 84
Eliot, Charles, 82
elk, antlers of, 52
endogenous rhythm, 52–54
Enteman, Mrs., 192
entomophilous flowers, 136
epilimnion, 107
equinox, vernal, 45–46
Eremotherium (ground sloth),
13–14
ermine, coat color of, 51
eutrophication, 109–13
evaporators, maple syrup, 38, 40–
43
evergreen habit of plants, 27–35

fall webworm, 65
Farrar, Edward R., 75
Federal Water Pollution Control
Act, 115
fieldstones, 56–59
firewood, 1–8
fish, lake quality and, 108–9, 111,
113
fleas: trap for, 26; water, 114
flies: apple maggot, 127, 129–30;
cherry fruit, 130; face, of cattle,
127; in composting toilet, 179;
tachinid, 76; tsetse, 128
flowers: albino, 16–25; anemophilous, 136; Boston ivy, 81;
cranberry, 152–53; effect of
day-length on, 51; entomophi-

lous, 136; poinsettia, 190; railroad dispersed, 118–20; spinach,
51; tobacco, 51
flypaper, 126–27
Fouqueria splendens (ocotillo), 33
foresters, definition of, 7
forget-me-not, pollen of, 134
fox grape, origin of, 152
Franklin, Benjamin, 47
frogs, arboreal, 199, 201
fruit: avocado, 9–15; Boston ivy,
81; cranberry, 153, 155–56;
dispersal by railroads, 119–20;
mulberry, 86–95
fungi: culture of, 165–74; pests
of cranberry, 153
fungus gardens, 167–72
Fusarium graminareum (fungus),
174

Gardner, Eliakim, 203–5
Garner, W. W., 50–51
geraniums, color preference in, 21–
22; on outhouses, 176
Gibbs, Jean, 159
glacial till, 58–59
glacier: and lakes, 107; and rocks,
58, 60, 63
glyptodonts, 14
gomphotheres, 14
grackles, and gypsy moths, 76
grasshoppers, trials of, 125
Grew, Nehemiah, 134–35
guests, working, 36–43
gypsy moths, 64–78, 129

Hall, Henry, 153
Halsted, Byron, 81
hamburgers, 196–98, 200
hay fever, 133–42
head lice (*Pediculus capitis*), 180–
88
Hechtl, Richard, 150
Helson, B. V., 130
hemlock (*Tsuga canadensis*): gypsy
moths and, 68; needle longevity,
30
Hogan, Ben, 149
holly, American (*Ilex opaca*), 30,
68

honeybees: pollen of, 140–42; sprays and, 70; stings of, 96–103

houseplants, 196–202

howler monkey, 199

hummingbirds, as pollinators, 23–24

hypolimnion, 107

indigo buntings, migration of, 50

injection therapy, 138

insects: cranberry pests, 153–54; in composting toilet, 179; pesticide resistance, 131, 187; repellants for, 29, 125; traps for, 126–32; trials of, 124–25

Integrated Pest Management, 131

introduced species: ailanthus, 90; Boston ivy, 80; gypsy moth, 64–78; railroads and, 118–22; starling, 73; white mulberry, 88–90

isoamyl acetate, 100

Ivy League, 79, 83

Japanese honeysuckle (*Lonicera japonica*), 119

Jerusalem artichoke, origin of, 152

judging of vegetables, 145–48

juncos, breeding of, 50

karesansui, 60–62

17-ketosteroid, seasonality of, 54

Kydonieus, Agis, 130

lakes, condition of, 106–16

larkspur (*Delphinium*), 23–24

Lawson, Charlene, 160

leafcutter ants, 166–74

leaf longevity, of plants, 27–35

Leucaena leucocephala, 8

lice, resurgence of, 180–88

liquid compost, 171

locust, black, 6, 68

log-splitters, 2–3

long-day plants, 51

Longland, David, 17–18

Lymantria dispar (gypsy moth), 64–78, 129

Macrauchenia, 14

Malpighi, Marcello, 134

mammoths, 14

manatees, 115

Mao Zedong, 4

maple: coppice of, 6; syrup, 38–43

marigold, white, 19–20

Mayo, Mrs. Thomas F., 74

mechanical harvesters, cranberry, 155–56

Merrill, Mr., 150

migration: bird, 48–50, 53; rock, 58–60, 62; salmon, 52

moles, and gypsy moths, 77

moon gardens, 22

moose, antlers of, 52

Morus (mulberry): *alba*, 86–95; *multicaulis*, 89–90; *nigra*, 91–92; *rubra*, 89, 93–94

mosquitos, 124, 130

mountain laurel (*Kalmia latifolia*), 30, 68

mouse, white-footed, and gypsy moths, 77

Mraz, Charles, 101

Muhlenbach, Viktor, 118–22

mulberries, 86–95

Multicaulis Craze, 90, 92

mushrooms, cultivation of, 165–74

nekton, 106

nitrogen, in lakes, 110–11

nits, 184–87

nuclear polyhedrosis virus, 76

nutrients: in avocados, 11; in bee pollen, 141; in composted sewage, 178; in fungi, 173–74; in lakes, 110–14; in leaves, 32; in mulberries, 94

oak: coppice of, 6; gypsy moth and, 67–68; hayfever and, 136, 138; live, 30

O'Connell, Jean, 159

ocotillo (*Fouqueria splendens*), 33

Oencyrtus kuvanae (wasp), 76

oligotrophic lakes, 106–9

onions, bulb formation of, 51
opossums, and gypsy moths, 77
oropendolas, 199
outhouses, 175–79

parrots, 199
Parthenocissus: quinquefolia, 80, 82; *tricuspidata*, 80–85
parthenogenesis: aphids, 52; cockroaches, 131
Paspalum dilatatum (Dallis grass), 119
pebbles, definition of, 56
pecan, origin of, 152
pediculosis, 181
pemmican, 152
Periplaneta americana, 123, 131
Perrin, Noel, 38
Perrotet, Georges Samuel, 89
Persea americana (avocado), 9–15
pest control, insect, 123–32; gypsy moth, 69–78; head lice, 186–87
Phalaenopsis violacea 'Alba', 22–23
pheromones, 128–129: bark beetle, 130; cockroach, 131; gypsy moth, 71–72, 78, 129; honeybee, 100
phosphorus, in lakes, 110, 114
photoperiodism, 50–54
photosynthesis, 28–34
phytoplankton, 107–8
pigments, in flowers, 18
pine: bristlecone (*P. aristata*), 30; foxtail (*P. balfouriana*), 30; white (*Pinus strobus*), 30, 68–69
pink, albino, 17
Pinus longaeva, 30
Pleistocene animals, 13–15
plica polonica, 184
Poinsett, Joel Roberts, 191
poinsettia (*Euphorbia pulcherrima*), 189–95
pollarding, 7
pollen, and hayfever, 134–42
pollination: by animals, 23–24, 136, 155, 202; by wind, 136–37

pollinia, 136
pollinosis, 133–42
Popenoe, Wilson, 11
population growth, effects of: on demand for protein, 173; on forests, 5; on lakes, 109–13
Potentilla argentea (silvery cinquefoil), 119
Price, Mary, 23
privies, 175–79
Prokopy, Ronald, 129
protein, fungal, 173–74
pumpkin, pollen of, 134

rabbits, snowshoe, coat color of, 51
raccoons, and gypsy moths, 77
ragweed, and hayfever, 136–37
railroad flora, 117–22
rain forest burger, 200
redbud, albino, 17
red-winged blackbirds: and gypsy moths, 77; migration of, 49
Resnick, Marlene, 160
rhinitis, seasonal, 133–42
robins, feeding of, 48
rocks, moving of, 55–63
rosebay (*Rhododendron maximum*), 30
rose fever, 134, 139
rose-shell azalea, albino, 17
rotenone, and fish, 113
Roth, Louis, 131
Rubenstein, Howard, 102–3
Rumex dentatus, 121

salmon, migration of, 52
Samia walkeri (moth), 90
Scheifflin, Eugene, 73
seam squirrels, 183
Secchi disk, 106, 110, 112
Secchi, Pietro Angelo, 106
seed catalogs, 17, 25
seed dispersal: avocados, 10–15; mulberries, 90; by railroad, 119–20
seed rocks, 58
Selasphorus platycercus, 23–24
short-day plants, 51
shrews, and gypsy moths, 77

silk, 87–91; gypsy moth, 66
silkworm (*Bombyx mori*) 72, 87–90
skunks, and gypsy moths, 77
sloths, 199; giant ground, 13–15
Smith, J. Russell, 93, 95
Snodgrass, Robert, 97
social distance, 185
solstice: summer, 46; winter, 44–45
sparrow, white-throated, migration of, 49–50
spinach, bolting of, 51
Spinney, Mrs. F. T., 73
spruce: Norway, 29; Sitka, 30
squirrels, and gypsy moths, 77
starlings and gypsy moths, 77; introduction of, 73
Stone, Eric, 163–64
stones, moving of, 56–63
stone walls, 57–58, 61, 63; burning of, 74; effect of ivy on, 84
stoves, wood, 2–5
stratification, lake, 107
strawberries, runners of, 51
sugarhouses, 38–43
summer catarrh, 133–42
summer diarrhea, 112
sunflower: exhibiting, 145; origin of, 152; pollen, 139
Surgeoner, G. A., 130
Swain, Elisabeth, 38–40, 123–24, 175, 195
swallows, migration of, 48–49
swimmer's ear, 112
synthetic cow's breath, 128

temple gardens, Japanese, 60–63
tent caterpillars, 65–66
Thorburn, Amerine, 160
thermocline, 107
toadflax (*Kickxia elatine*), 121
tobacco, flowering of, 51
tomatoes: exhibiting, 143–51; railroads and, 120
toucans, 199
Toxodon, 14
traps: bird, 50; insect, 71–72, 126–32
trees: destruction of, 198–201;

evergreen vs. deciduous, 26–35; firewood, 1–8; pollen of, 136–38; sugar from, 38–43
trillium, purple, albino, 17
trout, lake, 108–9, 113
Trouvelot, Leopold, 72–73
tsetse fly, 128
tulip tree (*Liriodendron*), 6, 68
typhus, louse-borne, 183

Uniform Time Act, 47–48
Upton, Everett, 149

Vaccinium macrocarpon, 152–64
vegetables, exhibiting, 144–51; railroads and, 119–20
venom, honeybee, 98–101
Verbena brasiliensis, 119
Viola pedata (bird's foot violet), 17
Virginia creeper, 80, 82
Vonk, Alice, 20
vulture, migration of, 49

Wade, Carlson, 140
Waser, Nickolas, 23
Wason, Fletcher, 150
wasps: parasitic, 76; stings of, 97–99, 102
water quality, 105–16
watermelons, exhibiting, 149
Webb, Ralph, 127
weeds, and railroads, 118–22
Wellington, Richard, 92
Welwitschia mirabilis, 30–31
White, E. B., 134
White, Elizabeth, 139–40
whiteflies, 127
white flowers, 16–25
Willett, William, 47
willows, for basketmaking, 6; hay-fever and, 137
Wilt disease, gypsy moth, 76
woodsman, definition of, 7

yews (*Taxus*), 30

Zeitgeber, 53
Zinsser, Hans, 183
zooplankton, 107–8